EUROPE'S CONSTITUTIONAL FUTURE

James M. Buchanan

Karl Otto Pöhl

Victoria Curzon Price

Frank Vibert

Introduction by
Graham Mather

IEA

Institute of Economic Affairs
1990

First published in December 1990
by
THE INSTITUTE OF ECONOMIC AFFAIRS
2 Lord North Street, Westminster, London SW1P 3LB

IEA Readings 33

ISSN 0305-814X
ISBN 0-255 36237-4 (paper)
ISBN 0-255 36238-2 (hard cover)

The Institute gratefully acknowledges financial support for its publications programme and other work from a generous benefaction by the late Alec and Beryl Warren.

Printed in Great Britain by
Goron Pro-Print Co. Ltd., Lancing, W. Sussex

Filmset in 'Berthold' Times Roman 11 on 12 point

EUROPE'S
CONSTITUTIONAL
FUTURE

CONTENTS

Contents

INTRODUCTION

Graham Mather
General Director,
Institute of Economic Affairs

EUROPE IS IN THE MIDST of its most profound period of change since the end of the last World War. The return of nationhood, political freedom and the market economy to Central and Eastern Europe marches alongside the achievement of a single market in the European Community. Now the agenda broadens and lengthens as the Community considers its shape and structure for the next phase of its development.

In Britain this process has been the cause of political tension and a debate that seems repeatedly to misfire. Britain seems cast in a negative, passive and reactive role in its European relations. A confused and unsatisfactory domestic debate is accompanied by clear under-performance as an effective influence on European development. To what can this lamentable position be attributed? Its consequences are as debilitating for this country's political economy as they are a loss to Europe as a whole.

In part it may have been the absence of a clear constitutional framework for the emerging Europe which has been the chief cause of tension and misunderstanding. In the common law tradition of limited powers, strict construction and well-understood divisions between broadly matching executives and legislatures, with a judiciary fulfilling a role of well-understood independence, the very dynamism of

European development on a different model may seem to pose a major challenge.

And, arguably, given the vested interests and political pressures which constantly confront market-opening and liberalisation, the dynamic opportunism of the European Commission's approach—most especially under the controversial, but clearly effective, leadership of President Delors—is both inevitable and necessary if progress is to be achieved.

It seems increasingly clear, however, that the structures which were fashioned for that phase of the Community's development are not appropriate for Europe's present and broader agenda. Because Economic and Monetary Union, however defined, involves a significantly greater role for Community institutions its constitutional and institutional structure is of paramount importance; indeed, it overshadows the purely economic debate.

More broadly, a Community which has influence or power over a wider agenda, and which is itself about to broaden its membership—for can it be doubted that a number of EFTA countries and former Communist nations will be in membership before the end of the century?—must address the more sophisticated checks and balances which become necessary.

If the 1980s were the years of the rediscovery of market economics, the 1990s will be the decade of constitutional and institutional development and reform. The opportunity to embark upon constitution-building is hugely exciting. It can draw from all the lessons of Britain's own political development, as well as the insights of modern understanding of the economics of politics, the critical role of sharply defined property rights, and a developed understanding of the relationship between economic choice and political freedom.

Given the rich resources of international constitutional and economic scholarship it is disappointing that so little work has been devoted to the models for a European constitutional settlement. The Institute of Economic Affairs is delighted in this pioneering volume to redress the position, and that the Nobel Laureate, Professor James Buchanan, should have agreed to set out in this book his vision of the benefits of an appropriate constitutional framework—benefits which, he argues, may draw from and improve on the American constitutional model.

In the context of Economic and Monetary Union, Dr Karl Otto Pöhl addresses in this book the extraordinarily difficult issue of how to achieve a non-inflationary European monetary policy capable of withstanding political pressures to loosen monetary discipline and which is nonetheless compatible with perceived requirements of democratic accountability.

It is notable that much of the EMU debate has focussed on monetary issues—the no less important economic considerations have been pushed to one side. Professor Victoria Curzon Price makes a most useful contribution to discussion by examining the competing economic philosophies which may come to fill this void, and her clear analysis illuminates an issue which will come to the forefront as the monetary debate is concluded.

For British readers Frank Vibert's thoroughgoing analysis and imaginative new proposals may provoke particular interest and discussion. He sets out the opportunities for building a vigorous and decentralised Europe based on co-operation in the European Council and Council of Ministers, using to the full the parliamentary frameworks of the member-states and moving away from the concept that Europe depends for its momentum on bureaucratic initiatives from the European Commission.

Britain does have the opportunity to equip herself quickly with a positive and constructive rôle in the new European structures. Britain can be the voice of free trade, the opponent of protectionism and trade blocs. Britain can be the bridge with the United States and its commercial and legal systems, and with Australasia and the dynamic new economies of the Pacific. For the EFTA countries and the re-emerging nations of post-Communist Europe, Britain can be spokesman, tribune and friend. For market liberals Britain can be a voice, and for pragmatists Britain can offer assistance in getting on with the practical job of building European systems that work.

To fulfil this role Britain will need to change. To be prepared to meet European methods of thinking and philosophical approaches halfway would help. But more important is the need for a pro-active approach: so that ideas compatible with market principles inform European debate early. Britain must be a year ahead of the debates, rather than six months behind at every stage. Civil servants must be re-programmed from reluctant implementers of German-derived directives to vigorous exporters of liberal free-market plans and policies. The many sources of intellectual and practical advance: think tanks, business organisations, professional bodies, learned societies, regulatory bodies, all will need to redouble their efforts to play an effective part in European policymaking if Britain's chronic under-representation of people and ideas in the European systems is to be corrected.

For its part, the Institute of Economic Affairs will continue to develop informed debate and discussion. It has already announced a programme of discussion meetings in Brussels designed to allow intellectual discussion of market-related issues before an audience of journalists, officials, Parliamentarians, business figures and other opinion formers. *Whose Europe?*, the Institute's most recent volume on European issues, has attracted wide and favourable attention and is in its second printing. *Europe's Constitutional Future* is a powerful and innovative addition to this work. The Institute never expresses a corporate view and must dissociate itself and its Trustees, Directors and Advisers from the views of the authors of this volume; it commends it as a particularly informed and imaginative contribution to debate and thanks the distinguished authors most warmly.

November 1990   GRAHAM MATHER

EUROPE'S CONSTITUTIONAL OPPORTUNITY

James M. Buchanan

Harris University Professor,
Center for Study of Public Choice,
George Mason University,
Fairfax, Virginia

I. INTRODUCTION

AT A 1986 CATO INSTITUTE CONFERENCE, I commended Professor Peter Bernholz for opening up a previously unexplored area for constitutional inquiry, an area that involves neither comparative analysis of alternative ideal designs nor attention to current constitutional change (Bernholz, 1986; Buchanan, 1986). Bernholz focussed on the potential for examining the characteristics of political régimes in the course of their historical development with a view towards identification of circumstances that might bring constitutional reform more closely to the realm of the politically possible. Bernholz suggested that there may exist phases in an historical sequence where a temporary convergence of interests makes a constitutional reform possible, settings that the political economist may identify and exploit in normative discourse.

Bernholz was directly concerned with prospects for reform in the monetary constitution, and I shall return to his more recent proposal in Section V. But my reason for reference to the earlier discussion is by way of introduction to the central thesis of this paper. I shall argue that Europe is now presented with an historically unique opportunity to achieve that greatness which has so long remained unrealised. Quite literally, the 1990s offer Europe a *once-in-history* opportunity, which, if seized, can promise greatness as defined in a mutually agreed-on dimensionality, but which, if missed, must promise disaster. I do not use the 'once-in-history' appellation carelessly. And it is because of the descriptive accuracy of this appellation that I am optimistic about Europe's future. The opportunity is so clear that the folly reflected in failure to seize it is not included even within my public choice perspective on politics and politicians.

A *constitution* that will embody the terms of the contract that the peoples of Europe must make, one with another, individually and as members of separate national-cultural communities, is a *sine qua non* of the whole enterprise. But there are constitutions and constitutions, and the terms of the contract must match the corresponding historical realities. The contract must be such as to ensure mutual gains-from-trade, the ultimate test for which is voluntary agreement on the terms. And such agreement will be forthcoming only if the parties to the contract (individually, both separately and in groups) are effectively guaranteed or protected against exploitation during periods subsequent to ratification.

Europe has a history of conflict among separately identified nation-states, each of which has commanded the loyalties of individual members. It is folly to expect a simple transference of these loyalties to 'Europe', conceptualised and romanticised as a supra-nation-state. The only constitutional structure that is consistent with the historically-constrained setting of the 1990s is that of a *federal union*, within which members of the separate units co-operate for the achievement of widely recognised and commonly shared objectives, those of internal (intra-European) peace and economic prosperity, within political arrangements that ensure individual liberties and, at the same time, allow for the maximal practicable achievement of standards of justice.

Lessons for Europe from US Experience

The Europe of the 1990s can learn lessons from the doomed experience of the USA, as Section II sets out in more detail. Europe can, under properly designed and historically relevant constitutional guarantees, ensure that the continuing advantages of the American structure are implemented and preserved while protecting against the tragically originated sequence of events that have undermined the attainment of the American ideal. In order to accomplish this grand design, which is available to Europe at this historical moment,

2

individual participants must rethink and reformulate their public political philosophy. They must recapture something of the mind-set of the 18th century. They must shed off all semblance of the Hegelian mythology in which the individual realised himself/herself fully only in the specific political community defined by the collectivity. This fountainhead of ideas for the socialist century, which spawned the 'fatal conceit' (Hayek, 1989) that socialism represented, must be categorically refuted, repudiated and rejected.

Fortunately, and here again the circumstances of current history must command attention, the momentous events of the 1980s in Eastern Europe and, indeed, throughout the world have served to shift public attitudes toward the philosophical reversals that seem required here. Section III sets out the argument in somewhat more detail.

As the discussion which follows in Section IV indicates, however, more is needed than the attainment of something akin to the 18th-century scepticism about the efficacy of politicised achievement of individuals' values. Such scepticism, standing alone, opens the door to interest-driven exploitation of the historically developed institutions of modern politics, to the epoch of 'politics without principle' or, in de Jasay's terminology, 'the churning state' (de Jasay, 1985). A public rediscovery of the romance of *laissez-faire* might suffice, but in Western Europe and America such a shift in attitudes seems beyond the possible. (Eastern Europe is an altogether different matter, and, indeed, the new-found faith in the efficacy of markets, defined in the negation of politicised direction, may well prove sufficient to ensure dramatic threshold leaps in economic well-being.) Again, however, appropriate constitutional design for a federal union can allow the predicted working of interest-driven utilisation of political agency to proceed so long as the limits to damages are constrained by effective competition among the separated polities of the inclusive federation.

In Section V, I illustrate the whole argument by reference to a European monetary constitution, and here I again build on the suggestions advanced by Bernholz. Section VI addresses some of the more general issues in summary, and, specifically, those that are involved in the German question. Finally, Section VII concludes the chapter with a defence of the prediction that Europe will, in the 1990s, establish an effective federal union.

The idea of *federalism*, of diversity among separate co-operative communities, of shared sovereignty, of effective devolution of political authority and, perhaps most importantly, of the *limits on* such

3

authority—this idea, enforced within credible *constitutional* guarantees, can be the European source of a fabulous century.

II. UNITED STATES, 1787—EUROPE, 1990[1]

Europe in 1990 finds itself historically positioned in a setting analogous to the United States in 1787. There are, of course, major differences as well as similarities, and analogies can always be overdrawn. But if attention is placed on the comparison between the unrealised opportunity that is (was) within the possible and the alternative future that failure to seize the opportunity would represent, the similarities surely overwhelm the differences.

In 1787, the citizens of the separate states in the American confederation shared the common experience of successful conflict with a colonial ruling government and, also, the failed effort at economic integration by the independent sovereign polities. To James Madison and his compatriots at Philadelphia, the confederation among the separate states was not enough, and the future prospect was one of continuing interstate economic conflict, described by economic autarky in a setting of increasing vulnerability of the separated states to external enemies. What was needed was a *constitution*, a set of rules that would restrict the sovereign authority of the states over citizens, and, at the same time, would establish a *central government* that would also command, directly, the loyalties of citizens.

Madison's grand design for the American federal union succeeded in its objective of creating and maintaining an open economy over the whole territory of the several states. The American economy, the effective extent of the market, came to be co-extensive with the external boundaries of the central government. Freedom of trade in goods, freedom of migration of persons, freedom of movement for capital, a common monetary unit—these characteristics ensured that the division of labour would be exploited to an internal maximum. And America, predictably, became rich.

But Madison's grand design for the federal union failed in its less recognised but ultimately much more important objective, that of limiting the range and scope of political authority over the liberties of citizens. In 1787, concern was centred on the potential abuses of authority by the separated states; the anti-Federalists were unsuccessful

---

[1] For a paper that treats the subject matter of this section at length, P. Aranson (1989).

in raising effective concerns about the potential authority of the central or federal government. After all, citizens of the states were creating a new government, the delegated powers of which were to be severely circumscribed. And, further, even as it exercised these delegated powers, Montesquieu's separational scheme was expected to provide further checks on over-extension. Madison's philosophy of federalism did not allow him even to dream of a federal Leviathan.

Right to Secede Implied in US Constitution

To the Founders in 1787, the fact that the citizens of the separate states were involved in creating a central government that would itself commence to share sovereignty with these creating states more or less carried with it the ultimate right of citizens in the separate units to secede from the federal union so established. And, indeed, had the question of secession been raised at all in the initial debates on the formation of the union, representatives of all the states would have dismissed it since the answer was, to them, self-evident. Without an implicit acceptance of an ultimate right to secede, to opt out, to exercise the exit option, the constitutional agreement hammered out in Philadelphia in the hot summer of 1787 would never have come into being at all.

If the advantages of economic union are so great, why should secession ever come to be in the interests of citizens of particular states in the federation? The potentiality of a viable secessionist threat could emerge only if the central government, through its internal decision structure, should take action that differentially damaged citizens of the separate states or regions within its territory. Should the central authority remain within the limits of actions defined by the 'general interest' of all its citizens, an effective argument for secession could never emerge from considerations of economic interest. This relationship may be stated obversely: the threat of potential secession offered a means of ensuring that the central government would, indeed, stay within those boundaries of political action defined by the general interests of all citizens in the inclusive territory.[2]

We may ask the hypothetical question: If the American constitutional agreement of 1787 should have included an effective

---

[2] For a technical argument, J. Buchanan and R. Faith (1987); for a general philosophical treatment, A. Buchanan (1989).

guarantee that the economy remain open, *externally* as well as internally, would the secession option have become viable to the coalition of Southern states in 1860? We can agree on the direction of effect. Secession from the federal union would have seemed less desirable to Southerners than, in fact, was the case in the presence of central government restriction on external trade.

I do not neglect the critical importance of the institution of human slavery for American constitutional history. The immorality of slavery provided the impetus for the formation and maintenance of regional coalitions, conflict among which generated both differentially damaging federal government trade restrictions and created the potential for southern secession, both of which may well have been counter to the strict economic interests of supporting citizenry. I emphasise only that this discussion is not an enterprise in American history but is, instead, an interpretation of some of that history that seems relevant to the European position in 1990.

'American Federalism' a Mockery

In this context, Lincoln's decision to fight to preserve union can be viewed as a breaking of the implicit contract that had established the federal structure. The ultimate victory ensured that secession was no longer a viable option for citizens of the separate states, individually or in coalition. In the absence of the threat of the exercise of the exit option, there then existed no effective limit to the expansion of the powers of the central government beyond those embodied in the formalised structure of constitutional rules. It was perhaps inevitable that, sooner or later, these formal limits would be violated, although we may speculate on whether or not the Madisonian structure might have survived in a time when there existed no generalised mind-set similar to that which described the socialist century. In any case, the history has been written. It is mockery to use 'federalism' or 'federal union' in descriptive reference to the United States of 1990, which is, of course, simply a very large nation-state.

The lessons of the American experience for the Europe of 1990 are clear. The citizens of the separated nation-states face an opportunity to enter into a federal union that can be an instrument for achieving the enormous gains of economic integration. In this respect, the parallel with the America of 1787 is direct. In the process of establishing an effective federal union, a central political authority must come into being with some sovereignty over citizens in all of the nation-states. But the ultimate powers of this central unit must be reckoned with, and checks must be included in the constitutional contract that defines the federal structure. The formal rules of such a contract will not, however, be sufficient, as the American experience so well demonstrates. There must also be some explicit acknowledgement, in the contract of establishment, of the rights of citizens in the separate units to secede from union, upon agreement of some designated supra-majority within the seceding jurisdiction.

As the American experience suggests, the advantages of union should be such that secession should never become a meaningful alternative for the citizenry of any unit or set of units. This result emerges, however, only if the central political authority is constitutionally prohibited from enacting policy measures that are unduly discriminatory in their impacts on the separate units. Recognition of this potentiality suggests, in turn, that the initial contract should provide guarantees of freedom for both internal and external trade, that is, for trade among all citizens and firms within the inclusive territory of union *and* for trade among citizens-firms within the territory of union and all parties outside these limits in so far as internal policy makes this possible.

III. PUBLIC PHILOSOPHY FOR EFFECTIVE FEDERAL UNION

If Europe is to seize its opportunity to constitute a genuine federal union, its citizens must arrive at a philosophical understanding of the relationships among themselves, as individuals, and the collectivities in which they participate as members, both those defined as the historically familiar nation-states and the emergent inclusive Europe, a philosophical understanding that is quite different from that which described the public philosophy of the Hegelian-influenced socialist century. By reference to a 'philosophical understanding' or 'public philosophy' of citizens, I do not suggest that the disputation of those who call themselves philosophers need reach the level of conscious public awareness. I suggest only that observed attitudes of individuals in confrontation with politically orchestrated alternatives find their origins, at least in part, in some abstracted and idealised model of social interaction, a model which may remain subconscious and which may, of course, contain internal contradictions.

For well over a century, political entrepreneurs found it profitable to

7

exploit the ideological precept that the individual comes to the full realisation of human potentiality only as a sharing participant in a collective, the aims for which are objectively determinate, whether by the working of the laws of history or by the light of scientific reason. That which was 'good' for the individual is defined externally to any internal calculus of personal interest or reason. From this precept followed two direct consequences. First, the range and scope for the exercise of individual autonomy through free and voluntary contractual interaction independent of collectivised control was progressively narrowed. Secondly, decision-making procedures for the collective were evaluated in terms of their efficacy in identifying the objectively existent 'goodness' or 'truth' for all participants. In this setting, it is evident that an informed élite may, even if it need not, be superior in its judgement to any majority coalition of the total electorate.

Naïve Romanticism of Socialism-Collectivism

I have deliberately generalised the capsule description of the prevalent public philosophy of the 'Hegelian epoch' to include both Marxian and non-Marxian variants of socialism-cum-collectivism. Central to both was the precept that autonomously derived or originated individual values are superseded by the objectively defined ideal that is potentially attainable only by the collective. The public philosophy of the long socialist century was marked by a dramatic loss of the 18th-century faith in the co-operative-contractual potential released by individual autonomy and by an accompanying acceptance of faith in the working of collective agency. The naïve romanticism of 19th- and 20th-century socialism may be difficult for some historians of the 1990s to understand. But the history of ideas is marked by an epoch during which politics, defined as the total working of collectivities, was assumed to be characterised by both benevolence and omniscience.

The presupposed superiority of collective over individual choice and action necessarily required that there exist some well-defined collective unit. Socialist direction and control of the use of resources could be implemented only through a collective unit that could meaningfully define the effective boundaries of 'the economy'. And it was perhaps historical accident that caused attention to be focussed, practically, on the emerging nation-states, and particularly as nationalistic sentiments arose to complement the collectivist attitudinal thrust.

The nation-state, through its political agents, was successful in placing individual citizens in a status of dependency, to varying degrees. This loss of independence was necessarily accompanied by the emergence of an artificial loyalty to the collective, which granted any and all access to economic value. So long as the collectivised structure seemed to work within very broad limits of tolerance, the public philosophy of individuals, as subjects, could hardly have been expected to include consideration of alternative arrangements.

As noted, however, the dependency-induced loyalties to collective agencies were, from the start, artificial. Public attitudes toward collectivist experiments had never matched the romanticised models described by the intellectuals and academicians, as promulgated and elaborated by interest-driven political entrepreneurs. Over the long term, a viable public philosophy for collectivism required a demonstration of tolerably successful performance along with an observation of a tolerably efficient bureaucracy. As we know, neither of these conditions was met, and the second half of the 20th century witnessed an erosion in citizen support, both for highly centralised collectivised régimes and for politicised overreaching in those nation-states that continued to allow considerable scope for individual autonomy.

Failures Generate Revolutions

The failure of the experiments in 'democratic socialism' in the 1950s, the Khrushchev revelations of Stalinist terror, the flawed welfare-state extensions of the 1960s, the inadequacies of Keynesian macro-management in the 1970s, the woeful performance of collectivised economies in meeting the minimal demands of citizens—these events compounded to generate the genuine revolutions of the late 1980s, revolutions that surprised even those who had never been deluded by the Hegelian mythology.

In 1990, the public philosophy of collectivism belongs to an historical epoch that is past. Political entrepreneurs can no longer exploit the Hegelian sublimation of the individual to a collective *zeitgeist* or the Marxian dialectic of class conflict. Citizens, in both Western and Eastern nation-states, are sceptical of politicised, collectivised nostrums for alleged societal ills. Political entrepreneurs move now to exploit the rediscovered precepts of liberty and autonomy. Although displaced by two centuries from its origins, the public philosophy that can make European federal union a reality seems well on the way to being in place in 1990, giving credence to my claim that Europe does, indeed, have its once-in-history opportunity.

IV. POLITICISATION, PROFITS AND RULES FOR
A COMPETITIVE CONSTITUTIONAL GAME

I have suggested that the public philosophy required for European federal union must embody considerable scepticism about the efficacy of collective arrangements to produce economic value, and notably as authority is lodged in nation-states. A socialist ideology could never countenance the genuine diminution of sovereignty that nation-states must experience, a diminution reflected in some transference to a supra-national central unit, to 'Europe', and the more important transference to the free play of competitive forces operating across and beyond national boundaries. I have suggested, in Section III, that such a required shift in public philosophy is well on the way to becoming a reality of the 1990s.

The implementation of this public philosophy in the effective establishment of a federal union faces the formidable task of superseding the institutional history. Much more is required here than the shift in ideas. Full recovery of the 18th-century mind-set concerning the proclivity and prospects of politics and politicians to 'do good' would not suffice to erase two centuries of experience, during which people came to seek out private profits or rents through manipulation of the political-governmental-bureaucratic structure, and, in the process, learned tools of a trade unheard of in earlier times. For well over a century, and throughout the world, private profits have been made at public (citizens') expense. We should hardly expect the rent-seekers to be deterred by any shift in the ideological currents.

As I have stated in a summary title for a different lecture, 'Socialism is dead, but Leviathan lives on'. Or, if you choose, substitute the word 'mercantilism' for 'Leviathan' in the sentence. The attempts by well-organised interest or pressure groups to use political means to secure differential gains at the expense of the general polity-economy will not disappear in the post-socialist epoch, and, indeed, such attempts may prove even more successful in the absence of an articulated collectivist alternative. Public scepticism of politics and politicians has not been accompanied by a re-acquisition of faith in *laissez-faire*, in the efficacy of markets when left alone within a framework of law.

We seem to have come full circle to the setting confronted by Adam Smith in 1776, when he felt it necessary to demonstrate the fallacies in the argument that wealth is enhanced by particularised political intervention into the workings of markets. But, for citizens of Europe, there is a difference worthy of notice. For a large national economy, such as the United States, we are indeed facing the same task as that addressed by Adam Smith, as I have argued elsewhere (Buchanan, 1988). It becomes imperative that the interest-driven political interferences with markets be constitutionally restricted. But Europe confronts a setting that will permit the rent-seeking pressures of modern democratic politics to be finessed, while, at the same time, ensuring that the damages inflicted by such pressures will be limited.

The 'European Difference'

The 'European difference' here lies, of course, in the juxtaposition between the historically familiar exercises of rent-seeking pressures *within* nation-states and the prospect for a constitution of federal union that will ensure *competition* among producers and consumers of goods and resources across the territory that encompasses the several nation-states. This juxtaposition makes possible the achievement of economic integration, and the promise of substantial wealth enhancement, without any necessity for direct political confrontation with those groups *inside* the separate national units that seek to remain inside the protection of mercantilist restriction. The independent efforts of interest groups, as they operate on and through the political processes within separate national economies, need not be explicitly prohibited by the constitution of the federal union. Nor need the responses of majority legislative coalitions to such efforts be expressly limited. So long as individuals and associations (firms) are protected by the constitution of the federal union in their liberties to purchase and to sell both producers' and consumers' goods freely throughout the territory of the union, particularised interferences with internal economic relationships within a single national unit will be policed with reasonable effectiveness by the forces of cross-national competition. Politically orchestrated regulatory activity will tend to be restricted to that which increases overall efficiency, as this criterion may be defined by the preferences of citizens.

The 'European difference' at this stage of history that I have emphasised here also remains important in that it facilitates a relatively painless transition for the institutionally relevant public bureaucracy. Existing agencies of nationally separate bureaucratic authority can be kept in place without nominal removal of their specific function to regulate specific sectors. There need be no overt shift of bureaucratic oversight authority from Bonn, London, Paris, or Rome to Brussels. The separate national bureaucracies can continue to exist and to

11

operate, but their genuine authority to exploit the citizenry will be forestalled, again by the competitive forces imposed by the constitutional guarantees of open markets across the federal union.

V. A MONETARY CONSTITUTION FOR EFFECTIVE EUROPEAN UNION

The theme of this chapter, and especially of Section IV above, can be illustrated by reference to the monetary reforms necessary for effective economic integration. Clearly, such integration is not possible if central or reserve banks of the separate nation-states continue to exercise autonomous fiat-issue powers under legal structures akin to those in existence in 1990. This proposition holds regardless of the degree of political independence of the separate central banks. Monetary 'integration' is a necessary element in a more comprehensive programme for effective European economic union. A change in the monetary 'constitution' of each of the co-operating nation-states is required, as has already been widely acknowledged.

If the opportunity to achieve effective federal union is to be seized, however, attention must be paid to the particular design of the institutional reforms to be proposed, discussed and, ultimately, implemented. If the sort of institutional change suggested should be such as to facilitate the desired economic integration but, at the same time, it should fail to embody protection against undesirable consequences along other dimensions, generalised arguments in support of integration may be weakened, if not destroyed. If the fiat-issue autonomy of the separate central banks is simply replaced by fiat-issue autonomy of a monolithic European central bank, with no constitutionally credible guarantee against instability in the value of the fiat unit, the directional thrust of the argument for change may be reversed.

There are alternative institutional-constitutional monetary structures that would, ideally, facilitate genuine economic integration and, at the same time, contain credible protection against undesired fluctuations in the value of money. Political economists engage in long-continued debates over the relative effectiveness of commodity-based monetary standards, the constitutional rules that dictate rates of growth in base money, and constitutionally guaranteed targeted objectives to be generated by the monetary authorities of the separate nation-states (Brennan and Buchanan, 1981). For the most part, however, these debates involve the examination of the working properties of the idealised arrangements with little or no attention to the problems that arise in bringing about the transition between those arrangements in being and those that are to be achieved.

Hayek's Competing Currencies for Effective Economic Integration

It is precisely at this point that the inquiry launched by Peter Bernholz, noted earlier, becomes relevant and prompts the question: Given the existence and history of quasi-autonomous, independent central banks of the separate nation-states in Europe, each of which possesses a monopoly of fiat issue within its national territory, does there exist one of the several proposed constitutional alternatives that dominates others when evaluated in terms of the minimisation of transitional problems? In the European setting of 1990, the answer to such a question seems clear, as Bernholz (1990) recognises. The monetary arrangements for effective economic integration that must be constitutionally established are those that closely resemble the competing-currency scheme, advanced earlier by F. A. Hayek (1976, 1978).

The constitutional provisions required here are simple and straight-forward, and they operate directly on the legal relationships among persons and only indirectly on the operation of the monetary authorities. Citizens of Europe, of each and all of the separate nation-states of the federal union, must be legally-constitutionally allowed to transact affairs, to make contracts enforceable in their own courts, in the monetary unit issued by the central bank of *any* of the nation-states of the union, including the discharge of all monetary obligations, and specifically the payment of taxes to any and all political authorities. If this right of each citizen is constitutionally protected, and explicitly so in a set of constitutional rules for Europe, there need be *no* accompanying directive to central banks included in the constitution. These banks, as they are separately organised in the nation-states, can continue to operate in nominal independence and autonomy, in accordance with policy criteria of their own choosing, and subject to whatever domestic pressures may arise in the separate states.

The potential competition among the central banks of the separate nation-states provides the disciplinary pressure that will offset the inflationary proclivity of fiat-issue authorities. Because individual citizens are constitutionally guaranteed the right to make enforceable contracts in any monetary unit of the union, an attempt by a single central bank, as a politicised agency, to levy an inflation tax on residents within the national territory would be doomed to failure. And predicting such results, no central bank will act to ensure that its own money issue falls into disuse.

Under this set of monetary arrangements, the bureaucracies of established central banks remain in place; no new bureaucracy of a 'European' central bank need be organised. Citizens will, presumably, continue to use nationally issued fiat currencies, as well as nationally designated units of account, for the bulk of domestic economic transactions. Over some period of transition, cross-national transactions might tend to be made in the monetary unit of the nation-state with the best repute as a standard of value, as publicly perceived. In the 1990s, this unit might come to be the D-Mark or, if Switzerland is a member of the federal union, the Swiss franc. As citizens come to recognise the value of their right to contract in any unit, however, there need be no continuation of a single dominant unit for cross-national transactions.

Constitutional protection against collusion on the part of the separate central banks in the union would, of course, be necessary.

VI. EUROPEAN FEDERALISM, GERMAN UNITY, AND THE OPENING OF EASTERN EUROPE

To this point, the momentous events of 1989 have not entered into my discussion of Europe's constitutional opportunity, and, further, no change in the argument would have been dictated had 1989 simply not happened. But the revolutions in Eastern Europe *did* take place in 1989, and any treatment of a prospective European federal union must, at a minimum, attempt to assess the influence of these changes. I shall examine separately the effects of two related issues, as these may bear on prospects for Europe's seizure of its once-in-history opportunity. I shall, first, discuss briefly questions of German re-unification. I shall then discuss, more generally, the predicted effects of the opening of Eastern European economies to increased economic interaction with Western Europe and other parts of the world.

In a Europe historically described by the existence of autonomous, *fully sovereign* nation-states, whether or not these units are observed to co-operate in economic, environmental, political, social and military matters, the lesson of history is surely one that prompts concern about the potential imbalance that might be created by a straightforward merger of the two Germanies. Self-determination, as an extension of the liberal principle of voluntary agreement among the parties directly involved, is acceptable only to the extent that significant spillover effects on other parties are absent. But it is important to recognise that the potential harms that a unified Germany could impose on other Europeans emerge largely, if not totally, from the maintenance of the Hegelian mind-set that presumes nation-states to exert full and undivided sovereignty over their resident citizens.

The federalised alternative, in which sovereignty is genuinely shared, did not enter into the political consciousness in the socialist-collectivist century, a consciousness that accepted the necessity of a monolithic, centralised control over economic and social relationships. In the post-socialist mind-set that seems ready to emerge, in Europe as elsewhere, federal union for Europe becomes a real prospect. And with a genuine federal structure of governance, the bases for the fears of a dominant Germany are substantially reduced. If the constitution for Europe that establishes the federal union effectively ensures that any national unit, be it large or small, must remain open to the competitive forces that operate over all the inclusive territory of the union, why should, say, the citizen of Portugal be concerned much about the size of his nation-state relative to that of Germany?

European Federalism and Fears of German Secession

As noted earlier, however, residual fears may remain that a large and unified Germany would ultimately seek secession from any European federalism established. The costs of secession due to the shrinkage in market size would be relatively small for a sufficiently large nation-state. Empirically, it is difficult to estimate how substantial such fears of future German secession may be among the European citizenry of the 1990s. If this barrier seems sufficient to prevent the establishment of European union, German political entrepreneurs should begin to consider the incorporation of East Germany as a separate member of the European federal union, without overt re-unification with West Germany.

Again, it should be recognised that the generalised German thrust or urge for re-unification stems, in part, from the collectivist mind-set imposed by the Hegelian mythology. In the public philosophy attuned to the realities of European federal union, the political dimension of the nation-state matters relatively little. If the nation-state, as organised, is to possess much less authority than that assumed by the collectivist-socialist model, there need be, on the one hand, less fear of dominance by large units, and, on the other, less demand for inclusion in the large units by those peoples historically associated territorially, culturally or linguistically.

The opening of Eastern Europe to increased market-like relationships with other parts of the world, and notably with Western Europe, enhances the prospect that a European federal union, as established, will itself remain more open to trade with citizens of non-member states than might otherwise have been the case. A closed European union, post-1992, which has been predicted by some anti-federalists and some American critics, seems less likely to be realised, subsequent to the revolutionary events of 1989.

Constitutional Guarantees of Free Trade?

As noted earlier, there is a persuasive argument in support of constitutional guarantees for free trade both internally and externally, that is, both among the nation-states of the federal union and between the union and other countries of the world. The internal free trade area may be sufficiently large to capture most if not all of the scale advantages of an extended market. But freedom for external trade serves the equally important function of ensuring that internal political coalitions among majorities of the separate member nation-states will not successfully exploit minorities, and especially as concentrated in particular member-units. A federal union made up of Western European member-states that would have confronted a closed Eastern Europe, as seemed to be the prospect prior to 1989, might have succumbed to the protectionist temptations to discriminate against trade with America and the Far East. But, post-1989, with Eastern European prospects for trade in goods, migration of labour, and outlets for investment open, the internal political incentives should have shifted substantially in favour of leaving the European market open externally.

Citizens of Western Europe, when considering themselves as participants in the grand design for effective federal union, do not seem likely to support the formation of a closed trading area that would, itself, provide incentives for Eastern European economic and political isolation, and especially when there may exist prospects for including new members of the federal union drawn from the nation-states of Eastern Europe.

VII. WILL AN EFFECTIVE EUROPEAN FEDERAL UNION BECOME A REALITY?

In discussing Europe's constitutional opportunity, I have not carefully separated three different issues. To this point, the *mélange* has involved some consideration of the possibility of federal union, the inferred desirability of implementing such a union within appropriate constitutional guarantees, and, finally, prediction that the citizens of Europe will, in the 1990s, seize their once-in-history opportunity. Controversy should arise primarily, if not exclusively, over the third of these elements of the discussion. There is, or should be, widespread agreement to the effect that European federal union is possible and that an appropriately designed constitution can contain guarantees sufficient to ensure that the gains from the integrated and extended market are secured while, at the same time, the liberties of all individuals of member-units are expanded. From this generalised agreement, the normative thrust in support of establishment of such union follows as a necessary consequence. In what follows in this section, I shall presuppose that the first two elements of the discussion are accepted. I shall limit further discussion to the third, that is, to *prediction*.

European Federal Union in the 1990s

I have predicted that citizens of the several nation-states of Western Europe, acting through their existing political agents and processes, will take advantage of the constitutional opportunity that this moment in history offers to them. A European federal union will be established in the 1990s, with constitutional guarantees that will prevent the emergence of a monolithic 'Europe', as a central political unit, that would take on control and regulatory functions characteristic of the socialist-collectivist régimes during the historical epoch that is ending. Existing national units will not be reduced to the status of provincial administrative districts or to subordinate positions resembling those occupied by the American states in the post-Lincoln United States.

Those who have predicted that, upon any movement toward federal union, the central state, 'Europe', must assume critical dominance, and that Brussels, or the Brussels bureaucracy, will reduce national political agencies to submission are, I think, wrong. I base my contrary prediction on the particular convergence of ideas and events at the end of this century. As noted, the romanticised myth of the benevolent and

17

omniscient state came to influence public perception of politics in application to the existence of the separately sovereign nation-states of modern Europe. The romantic myth has been substantially displaced in the public consciousness of the 1990s, and there are no longer philosophers around who promote its revival. Nowhere in the world, East or West, do we find, in the 1990s, the naïve faith in collectivist nostrums that characterised both intellectual and public attitudes for most of the 19th and 20th centuries.

A central European state that would come to share sovereignty with the separate national member-units in a federal union, could not, therefore, be expected to capture and to command loyalties even remotely akin to those exploited so tragically by the nation-states of the last two centuries. The central polity of Europe, in a federal structure, would be required to emerge, grow and survive in an attitudinal climate that embodies generalised scepticism about both the motives of political agents and the workings of political institutions, at all levels. An additional difficulty that would be faced by a central European state in seeking to take on powers reserved to member-polities in a constitutional federal union lies in the continued residues of sentiment defined by shared historical experience, by cultural, linguistic and ethnic homogeneity. Citizens of European federalism will, indeed, come to think of themselves as 'Europeans', but they will scarcely stop thinking of themselves as British, French, German or Italian. Brussels, as the capital city of the federal union, would be expected to be more like Bern, in the Swiss confederation, than like Paris, in post-Napoleonic France.

The Dangers of Regulatory 'Brusselsisation'

My prediction may, of course, be falsified. If the proponents of federal union have not themselves fully escaped from residual socialist failures to understand the efficiency-generating forces of competition, both in markets for goods and among separately existing units in a federal system, they may advance nightmare versions of a regulatory 'Brusselsisation' that would prove totally unacceptable to those who are reluctant to surrender any shares in national sovereignty. And the power of the incentives offered to prospective rent-seekers by any prospective establishment of a Europeanised bureaucracy should never be underestimated. Excessive Europe-wide regulations, controls, fiscal harmonisation, fiat-issue monopoly, and so on, would, of course, destroy much of the gain that economic integration might promise. In this case, the failure of the whole effort would be reflected in pressures from the separate national units to secede, if indeed the federal union itself should ever come to be established. Reversion to the *status quo* prior to the 1990s becomes the scenario of failure.

The task of designing, in detail, the *constitution* for an effective federal union for Europe is formidable, and this task has scarcely been commenced. But I emphasise again that the opportunity is in place; the time is ripe. Europe waits for its own James Madison, who understands the constitutional economics of competition, and who, at the same time, appreciates the nuances of persuasive argument, bargaining and compromise required to generate agreement among apparently divergent interests.

Europeans, generally, must be convinced that establishment of a constitutionally defined federal union is a positive-sum movement for all parties. Finally, to end this chapter where it started, Europeans generally, including the James Madison of the 1990s, must recognise the propitiousness of this moment in the world's history.

REFERENCES

Aranson, P. (1989): 'The European Economic Community: Lessons from America', Paper for conference in Aix-en-Province; Duplicated, Emory University, Atlanta, Georgia, 1989.

Bernholz, P. (1986): 'The Implementation and Maintenance of a Monetary Constitution', *CATO Journal*, 6 (Fall), pp. 477-511.

———— (1990): 'Institutional Requirements for Stable Money in an Integrated World Economy', Paper for London Monetary Conference on Global Monetary Order, 1990; Duplicated, University of Basel, Switzerland, 1990.

Brennan, H. G. and J. M. Buchanan (1981): *Monopoly in Money and Inflation*, Hobart Paper No. 88, London: Institute of Economic Affairs.

Buchanan, A. (1989): 'Liberalism and the Right to Secede', Duplicated, Tucson, Arizona: University of Arizona.

Buchanan, J. M. (1988): 'Constitutional Imperatives for the 1990s', in

A. Anderson and D. Bark (eds.), *Thinking About America: The United States in the 1990s*, Stanford: Hoover Institution, pp. 253-64.

Buchanan, J. M. and R. Faith (1987): 'Secession and the Limits of Taxation: Towards a Theory of Internal Exit', *American Economic Review*, Vol. 77, No. 5 (December), pp. 1,023-31.

Hayek, F. A. (1976, 1978): *Denationalisation of Money*, Hobart Paper (Special) No. 70, London: Institute of Economic Affairs.

————— (1989): *The Fatal Conceit*, London: Routledge & Kegan Paul; Chicago: University of Chicago Press.

de Jasay, A. (1985): *The State*, New York: Basil Blackwell, Inc.

TWO MONETARY UNIONS – THE BUNDESBANK'S VIEW*

Dr Karl Otto Pöhl

President, Deutsche Bundesbank

I. GERMAN RE-UNIFICATION AND THE ROLE OF THE DEUTSCHEMARK

As I SPEAK TO YOU TODAY two important, even historic, events are unfolding before our eyes: the Economic, Monetary and Social Unification of the two Germanys (GEMSU), and the start of stage one of the planned European Economic and Monetary Union (EMU). Accident, not design, has these two events falling on the same date. But they are not wholly unrelated, since the unification of Germany is likely to speed up the European integration process. It is also true, however, that the two operations each have their own very distinctive features and will for the most part move forward under their own momentum.

What we see happening now in the GDR is the introduction of the Deutschemark in all its currency functions under the sole responsibility of the Bundesbank, and the adoption of market mechanisms in place of central planning. The introduction of the D-Mark is rightly seen as a powerful stimulant and at the same time as the trade-mark

---

*The Third IEA Special Lecture, delivered at the Queen Elizabeth II Conference Centre, London, on 2 July 1990.

and token of success of the unification process. European Economic and Monetary Union, by contrast, will imply the eventual replacement of all national currencies, including the D-Mark, by a single European currency issued, and its value controlled, by a common institution. These are two very important distinguishing features.

Like most economic experts, including those of the Federal Government, I would have preferred a step-by-step approach to German unification. But the urgency of the situation dictated otherwise. With hindsight, there can hardly be any doubt now that German economic, monetary and social unification was at the same time inevitable, necessary and desirable: inevitable, because the opening of the Berlin Wall left those looking for a better economic future with a chance to leave the GDR, thus burdening both states with incalculable costs without any corresponding benefits in sight; it was necessary, because only economic, monetary and social unification offered the prospect of a rapid and irreversible process of economic and social improvement in the GDR; and it was desirable, because it became clearer every day that economic and monetary unification would soon be followed by political unification.

The main elements of German Economic, Monetary and Social Union as they are incorporated in the State Treaty concluded between the Federal Republic and the GDR are public knowledge by now. From the point of view of the Bundesbank, two features are central:

o *First*, from 1 July the Bundesbank has been in full control of monetary conditions in the GDR as well as in the Federal Republic of Germany. The necessary institutional and technical arrangements are in place. Even if the pursuit of our monetary target will prove somewhat more difficult initially, this would not materially affect the Bundesbank's ability to stay its course of price stability.

o *Secondly*, the conversion arrangements finally adopted have effectively reduced the risks of entering the new phase with a large monetary overhang. The various conversion rates translate into an overall conversion factor of about 1·8 to 1, which is very close to what the Bundesbank initially proposed. The latest indications are that people will not spend too large a proportion of their new D-Mark holdings right away. This will clearly help to keep inflationary dangers in check. Monetary expansion in the Federal Republic is currently well under control, with M3 in the Federal Republic expanding at an annual rate of about 4 per cent. We calculate that

M3 will increase by about 10 per cent initially through introducing the D-Mark in the GDR; this corresponds well to the added economic potential.

Long-Term Benefits of German Re-Unification

You will not expect me to stress the risks of the exercise unduly. We are condemned to success in a situation such as this. The initial costs will be substantial, but the benefits to be gained after a difficult, perhaps even turbulent, initial phase will be well worth the effort. The benefits will not only accrue to my own countrymen and women, but to others as well, especially in Europe. The European Commission and others have raised their growth estimates for the German economy, but also for the Community as a whole, by a substantial margin. The long-term benefits to other countries could well be enhanced if the invitation to participate in the process of economic and political reconstruction that is under way in the GDR as well as other Eastern European countries is taken up by firms in our partner countries. Indeed, what will happen in the GDR is likely to serve as a model for other countries in Eastern Europe that are embarking on the transformation from planned to market-type economies. Their own efforts will be crucial to the success of the process, but success will also depend on the willingness of their Western partners to assist them.

Returning briefly to some of the implications of GEMSU, you will recall that already months ago financial market analysts made their back-of-the-envelope calculations and quickly concluded that German interest rates would have to rise substantially, and that this would pull up global interest rates. As so often, markets reacted ahead of time, long before the costs could be estimated with any precision. We know now that the net public sector borrowing requirement in Germany will increase substantially. For the whole of this year, it is estimated at about 80 billion D-Mark, and for 1991 at about 100 billion D-Mark. These totals include deficits incurred by public authorities in the GDR, to be financed through borrowing in the German capital market either directly or through the German Unity Fund. (They exclude certain items relating to the future operations of the new Trust Fund set up to re-organise and re-privatise state-owned companies and other state property.) Altogether, on this basis, public sector borrowing will grow to the equivalent of about 3·5 per cent of GNP, starting from the very low level of less than 1 per cent of GNP in 1989. However, the totals must be judged in relation to the size of our capital market and the high saving propensity of our household sector. Total net savings in Germany amounted to some 310 billion D-Mark in 1989, 100 billion D-Mark of which had their counterpart in our large current account surplus. Nevertheless, public sector borrowing of the size envisaged for 1990 and 1991 can be justified only temporarily and in the light of the exceptional circumstances in which it will arise. The Bundesbank has repeatedly emphasised the potential implications for interest rates of sharply higher borrowing by the public sector. It is our strong view that the large, unavoidable transfer of public funds to what is now the GDR should at least in good part be offset by re-structuring public expenditure. The unification process offers ample scope for cuts in certain expenditure areas that relate to the division of Germany in past decades.

High Interest Rates Inevitable

If interest rates, both nominal and real, in the industrial world are currently at very high levels, this is, of course, not only the consequence of a larger demand for capital in Germany. Other reasons also account for this, as is well known. Indeed, the fact that interest rates are as high as they are should in my view not be a matter for undue concern. The industrial world is on a sound growth path. Real growth is proceeding at very satisfactory rates not only in Japan and the rest of the Asian economy, but also in Europe. If it is somewhat more moderate in North America, this seems to be quite in line with adjustment needs. The world's savings/investment balance is likely to remain under strain. Relatively high interest rates, both nominal and real, are in these circumstances largely unavoidable. They are indeed a means of ensuring that non-inflationary economic balance is maintained.

Greater calls on available financial and real resources in the context of GEMSU are likely to reduce our large trade and current account surpluses. This would clearly be in our own interest, as it would help to keep inflationary pressures under better control. But it would also be desirable from the point of view of international payments adjustment.

Most experts expect the decline of Germany's huge current account surplus to be relatively slow. Indeed, German exporters will not want to give up hard-won world markets lightly, and they will be even less inclined to do so if export orders keep coming in as before. This is one reason why a good response on the part of imports to the additional consumer and investment demand generated by German economic unification would be highly desirable; indeed, rising imports should ideally make the major contribution to reducing our surpluses. But this too depends on demand pressures in the potential exporting countries being reduced. In not a few cases, the needed policy responses would seem highly appropriate in any case to avert the risk of domestic inflation accelerating again.

There is a wide measure of agreement, based on sound economic analysis, that the exchange rate of the D-Mark should be strong in the period ahead, so as to facilitate the adjustment that is called for. A strong D-Mark has been our aim all along, even though we have not pursued specific exchange-rate targets as part of our economic or monetary policy. It was to be expected that the D-Mark would fluctuate up and down, as news relating to the unification process is being evaluated from day to day in the exchange markets. But we have not been unduly concerned about the short-term behaviour of the D-Mark in recent months, even though it has at times been tending to move in a lower range within the ERM band than we might have liked to see, while remaining relatively strong against many other currencies, including sterling. The increase in our market interest rates has helped the relative strength of the D-Mark, as has the 'pre-emptive' rise in our official rates and the decline in short-term rates in some partner countries.

I am confident that home-made price and cost pressures will remain well under control even in the more difficult circumstances confronting us. On present indications, the rate of inflation in Germany will remain below 3 per cent a year in 1990, as it was in 1989. This I think is a remarkable result, given that we are now in the eighth year of an economic expansion, with real growth of about 4 per cent a year in 1989 and 1990.

Inflation Rate Differentials in Europe

I do not see any likelihood of a sharp acceleration of prices in 1991. I am, however, somewhat concerned that on this basis the inflation differential in our favour *vis-à-vis* some other countries will continue as before, or may even grow somewhat wider again as inflation rates tend to rise here and there. Inflation rates are ranging at present between 2 per cent and 7 per cent a year within the Exchange Rate Mechanism, and between 2 per cent and 18 per cent a year within the EMS taken as a whole. These large inflation differentials are clear evidence of manifest shortfalls in economic policy performance in a number of

Community countries. With exchange-rate adjustments being effectively constrained, not only within the Exchange Rate Mechanism, serious policy dilemmas are bound to arise. The virtual absence of any exchange-rate risk over long periods tends to attract capital flows to countries with relatively high nominal interest rates, thus strengthening their exchange rates, but also frustrating efforts to contain home-made inflationary pressures through monetary policy action. In time this will result in a loss of competitiveness for parts of their industry that may prove difficult to reverse. In the low-inflation countries, the inflexibility or—even worse—a real depreciation of the exchange rate risks causing inflationary impulses being imported from abroad. This must be a matter of concern, for partner countries individually and for the system as a whole.

In recent years, a strong D-Mark, and the economic and monetary policy that stands behind it, has served as an anchor of stability for other partner countries' economic and monetary policies in the EMS and beyond. This anchor rôle has been bestowed upon us, it is not ours by design, even though it was to be foreseen that the D-Mark would play a major rôle as an intervention currency and as a reference point for other currencies participating in the system. It is the consequence of policy choices made elsewhere as a matter of convenience. The recent decision of Belgium to tie its currency even closer to the D-Mark than before is only the latest example. I take it as a vote of confidence in our own ability to see the D-Mark continue in its rôle as a stability anchor in Europe. Our partners in the EMS, and particularly those participating in the Exchange Rate Mechanism, have recognised all along that anchoring to the D-Mark does not amount to a soft option. This will, of course, also hold true for Britain, once sterling comes under the rules of the Exchange Rate Mechanism, which I expect to be the case soon—'when the time is right'. The Governor of the Bank of England has rightly stressed recently that this should not be seen as a soft option.

II. THE LONGER VIEW: TOWARDS EMU

Taking a somewhat longer view, I would also warn against all temptations to incorporate into the project of European Economic and Monetary Union elements that would amount to a soft option. The Delors Report stressed three principles to be respected: plurality, subsidiarity and parallelism. The report saw a need to take account of the diverse social, cultural and political conditions in the member countries; to limit Community responsibilities to those essential to the functioning of economic and monetary union; and to advance in parallel on the economic and monetary fronts. These are sound principles.

I am concerned that parallel progress towards economic and monetary union may not be assured, as commitments in the area of budgetary policy remain vague. Fiscal discipline supported by clearly formulated rules of behaviour, especially in so far as they relate to the size of fiscal deficits and their financing, are at the centre of the issue. If such rules of budgetary discipline prove superfluous at some future stage because self-discipline together with market discipline prove effective, all the better for it. But experience so far in the Community and elsewhere does not justify overly high expectations.

I am even more concerned that the principle of subsidiarity should not be applied in areas where it would clearly be misplaced. *Subsidiarity definitely has no place in the realm of monetary policy. Monetary policy cannot be subdivided; it has to be of one piece.* Responsibility for it can only be placed either at Community level, that is with a European Central Bank System (ECBS)—or whatever is to be its name—empowered to pursue price stability as its primary objective, or with the competent national authorities, that is, with national central banks. As you know, the European Council has already decided in favour of the establishment of a European Central Bank System, and the Intergovernmental Conference which is to start in December will have to agree on a Statute for this new Community institution as part of its negotiating tasks.

Blueprint for an ECBS Statute

I welcome the fact that the Committee of EEC Central Bank Governors has been asked to submit a blueprint for a Statute of the future ECBS. There is already a wide measure of agreement among the Governors that the ECBS would have to be fully in charge of monetary policy in the Community if it is to attain its primary objective, price stability. The notion of a European Central Bank determining the broad guidelines for monetary policy in the Community, and national central banks implementing them with a large degree of freedom in accordance with the special circumstances of their national economies and the needs of their financial markets, would in my view be unacceptable as a basis to build on. What would be the guidelines laid down at European Central Bank level? What powers to see them properly implemented would the European Central Bank have, if this is to be called a European Central Bank System worthy of the name?

Even though, for well-understood reasons, the ECBS would in all likelihood have a federal structure, with one central bank per member, the central element would have to be strong enough to assure policy consistency and operational efficiency. A strong central element would also underpin the independence of the system from Community and Government interference. As members of the Governing Board of an ECBS, the national central bank governors will be expected to act without any national mandate, responsible only to the objectives laid down in the ECBS Statute and to its rules-book. It would nevertheless be wise to have a strong central element, call it a Directorate or otherwise, whose members would be an integral part of the Governing Board and would in the nature of things give added force to the system's autonomy in the day-to-day performance of its task.

The framework of the ECBS as outlined in more detail in my Paris lecture,[1] and the distribution of tasks, does not rule out the possibility that certain responsibilities that are not central to the pursuit of a consistent monetary policy could be left in the hands of national central banks acting as the operational arm of the system. The settlement of payments, open-market operations with the banks, business on behalf of government institutions and the like could well be taken care of by the national central banks—acting in accordance with the guidelines and instructions of the ECBS. In addition, the national central banks should, in my opinion, be made responsible for bank and stock exchange supervision where this is not already the case, as, for example, in the Federal Republic of Germany. This means that the national central banks would play a rôle similar to that of the Federal Reserve Banks in the United States or the Land Central Banks in the Federal Republic of Germany. However, they (and/or the finance ministers!) would have to give up their right to formulate independent national monetary policies. Particularly for Germany, this would have far-reaching implications. The Central Bank Council, which today is the supreme decision-making body in monetary policy, would lose its most important function, a consequence which may not have become quite clear to every advocate of an ECBS in the Federal Republic of Germany.

---

[1] 'Basic Features of a European Monetary Order', Paris, 16 January 1990.

Controversy over ECBS in Britain

I am aware that the issues relating to the status of a future European Central Bank System are hotly debated in this country. I believe I understand the arguments put forward against central bank autonomy, based as they are on the fact that your unwritten constitution vests all power ultimately in Parliament, including that over monetary policy. Experience in my own country and in not a few other countries clearly supports the case for central bank autonomy in its special area of competence.[2] It seems to me that in the context of European Economic and Monetary Union an even stronger case can be made for the political autonomy of a future ECBS than at our own national level. For one thing, a number of factors working in favour of monetary discipline, including those deriving from past experience of inflation and its evil consequences, may be less strong in the Community, for a variety of reasons. For another, the constant need for compromises to be sought at the political level would work to the detriment of an effective and stability-oriented monetary policy, if it were allowed to force it way into the area of central banking. I believe a high degree of autonomy bestowed upon an ECBS in its sphere of competence should not be equated with lack of accountability. If there is agreement that inflation is democracy's enemy No. 1, success in ensuring price stability should be taken as adequate testimony to the central bank's accountability.

I believe that the future ECBS should also be responsible for the management of the foreign currency reserves and for intervention in the exchange markets, subject to any agreements that may be concluded at government or Community level involving the exchange-rate régime. The ECBS would, of course, have an important rôle in any such agreement for the simple reason that commitments in the area of exchange rates and intervention have direct implications for monetary policy. It is important that operations in foreign exchange markets should not undermine the central objective of price stability.

Economic Convergence at Two Speeds

Allow me to use this opportunity to comment briefly on the debate about what has become known as integration at two speeds. I was

---

[2] Alan Greenspan in a speech before the Subcommittee on Domestic Monetary Policy on 25 October 1989: '. . . independence enables the central bank to resist short-term inflationary biases that might be inherent in some aspects of the political process. The Federal Reserve must take actions that, while sometimes unpopular in the short run, are in the long run in the best interest of the country.'

surprised that a brief remark I made after the last ECOFIN Council meeting in Luxembourg attracted much greater attention than it deserved. I merely recalled some of the conclusions of the Delors Committee with respect to those countries that may not initially be prepared, or be in a position, to subject their monetary policies to the strict discipline of a European Central Bank System. Without questioning the consensus on the final objectives of the Community, as well as full participation by all members in the same set of institutions, the Delors Report stated that a degree of flexibility should be maintained concerning the date and conditions on which some member-countries would join certain arrangements.

In fact, this statement only confirms what has been practised so far within the European Monetary System and in other EC areas. The agreement reached at Schengen on border controls and related matters is only the latest example. It was in this context that I mentioned France, the Benelux countries and my own country as an example of the high degree of economic convergence which has meanwhile been reached among them. It goes without saying that this convergence is an essential prerequisite for the final fixing of exchange rates, which is a *conditio sine qua non* of monetary union.

III. THE ROLE OF THE ECU

I should also like to take this opportunity to say a word about another subject, which is that of the ECU and its rôle. I shall not comment at length on the detailed proposals made recently by the British authorities, as these will be discussed in the appropriate forums in the coming weeks. I have, of course, taken note of them with great interest. Whatever the reactions of other partners to the proposals, the mere fact that they have been put on the table for discussion should be welcomed. Indeed, no idea put forward should be dismissed outright. So, with this introduction allow me to make a few remarks on the ECU issue of a more general nature.

The ECU was created as a basket of currencies. This helped its development as a hedging instrument in the private ECU area, so long as exchange rates proved to be extremely volatile both within the EMS and against the US dollar. The ECU has also gained some prominence as an instrument for other financial market purposes. It is widely viewed as a currency by market operators, even though it still lacks some of the essential features of a currency. The ECU has, by contrast, not assumed an important rôle as an official reserve and settlement instrument. It surely is not at the centre of the EMS. This has been a cause of disappointment and regret on the part of ECU enthusiasts, as well as of others.

The Delors Report gave the ECU little space, though it acknowledged its financial market rôle and its potential for being developed into the common currency of a final EMU, provided it could be adapted to the new rôle. This would mean giving up its basket character in favour of an ECU *sui generis*. This, I understand, is what the new British proposals aim at, although at the outset they could also be applied to the existing ECU.

Dangers of a European Parallel Currency

As the Delors Report pointed out, there are potential dangers to monetary policy in creating an additional currency that would circulate alongside national currencies as a parallel currency. One danger would lie in the pressures that would undoubtedly arise to expand the issuance of the ECU currency over time to give it greater prominence. The constant demands made for the promotion of the existing ECU and its rôle provide enough indication of the kind of pressures to be expected. So do—in another context, that of the IMF—the constant demands to create SDRs in the expectation that reserve holdings in national currencies would then be reduced by a corresponding amount.

The key element in the management of a currency must be the maintenance of its value, not the promotion of its use. The present ECU's rôle in the financial market no doubt has been enhanced by the help it receives from Community and national authorities, some of it at the expense of the taxpayer and without any clearly demonstrated benefit, except to the operators in the market. Indeed—all other things being equal—assuming that private issuers and investors in ECU instruments pursue their profit incentives, the pace at which the market for such instruments expands must in good part be a function of the willingness of Community or national public issuers to offer attractive conditions, at least at the margin, relative to those available in national currencies.

The most recent proposals would see ECUs issued as a dual currency by a European Monetary Fund (EMF) owned by the national central banks. Central banks would be obliged to ensure convertibility of their currencies into the ECU on demand and at exchange rates that

31

would be either fixed from the start or allowed to move only within very narrow bands. This would be expected to impose discipline on monetary policies in the participating countries, with the ECU serving as a European standard in much the same way as the old gold standard is said to have worked. At the same time, national central banks would remain accountable to national political authorities. The authors see it as an advantage that their proposal would preserve the principle of subsidiarity, enhance the prospects for price stability and maintain competition among national monetary policies, in fact adding a new element to such competition through the ECU currency.

Nevertheless, in some key aspects, the new proposals follow the original ideas underlying the concept of a second 'institutional phase' of the EMS: creation of ECUs against national currency, establishment of an EMF with tasks of its own, including intervention in third currencies, etc. With the adoption of European Economic and Monetary Union as a Community objective and its inclusion in the EEC Treaty under the 'Single Act', we have moved far beyond the concept of a second 'institutional phase' of the EMS.

Price Stability the Primary Objective of Monetary Policy

The revised 'Council Decision on Closer Co-operation between Central Banks of Member States', adopted in March 1990, recognises price stability as the primary objective of monetary policy, and as being essential to the permanent achievement of exchange-rate stability. The closer co-operation among Community central banks which we are now organising is to serve this objective. I consider this a major new crossroads from which to move forward to Economic and Monetary Union. Without it, the main focus would remain on the stability of exchange-rate relationships. This would confront countries seeking greater price stability than others with familiar monetary policy conflicts that could be resolved only by parity changes from time to time. If Economic and Monetary Union is to be the goal, the commitment to price stability is indeed essential and must be vested in a European Central Bank System empowered to pursue it independently of instructions from Community or national authorities. Without a clear assignment of responsibilities, the commitment to price stability would lack credibility.

It has been rightly argued that a common currency is not an essential element of monetary union. In my own view, a common currency would in the end still be desirable to demonstrate the irreversibility of the process and give the Union its own identity. It will be some time yet before we come to that point. Rather than adding to the problems that we will have to overcome on the way to that final step, we should seek to ensure that cohesion between national economies and their currencies will be strengthened, so as to prepare for the moment when exchange rates can be fixed permanently. Then is the time to decide on the creation of the new common currency that will replace the national currencies. Then will this be the logical step to take, with the new ECBS firmly installed to exercise the necessary control over a common monetary policy.

As the President of the Dutch central bank, Wim Duisenberg, stated in his written contribution on the subject of a parallel ECU currency to the work of the Delors Group:

> 'Economic and monetary union requires economic convergence and the acceptance of the loss of sovereignty implicit in the abolition of the exchange rate as an adjustment instrument. The development of the ECU into an international currency used in parallel to national currencies cannot enable us to avoid this requirement nor can it facilitate its realisation.'[3]

---

[3] W. F. Duisenberg, 'The ECU as a parallel currency', *Delors Report*, 1989, p. 189.

TOWARDS MONETARY UNION IN EUROPE*

Dr Karl Otto Pöhl

President, Deutsche Bundesbank

I WAS HAPPY to accept the invitation to speak to you on the occasion of your General Meeting, since it seems to me that no other country owes more to the liberal spirit which informs your Society than does the Federal Republic of Germany. Men like Eucken and Müller-Armack, Hayek and Röpke—to name but a few—created the intellectual basis for West Germany's spectacular economic successes in the post-war years—successes which are inseparably associated with the name of Ludwig Erhard. Today we are witnessing the collapse of the socialist counter-model—a really historic change, and, like Goethe (as an eye-witness of the battle of Valmy), we can say 'we have been there to see it'.

The structural changes in Eastern Europe and what is still (until 3 October 1990) the GDR are proving rather painful—nothing else, after all, was to be expected—but they are irreversible and will alter the face of Europe in the future. It seems to me that conceptual inferences should be drawn from them for European integration, and I think your conference can make a major contribution to that end.

As far as the monetary policy side of European integration is

---

*Speech delivered to a luncheon meeting during the 1990 General Meeting of the Mont Pelerin Society in Munich, West Germany, 3 September 1990.

concerned—and, in view of the short time available, I should like to confine myself to this aspect—one may wonder whether institutional changes extending as far as the creation of a European currency and a European central bank are really quite as indispensable as they are made out to be in some quarters. Even before the establishment of an intra-German monetary union, I voiced the opinion that, first of all, it is better to gain experience of what is known as stage one of European economic and monetary union before more far-reaching steps are contemplated. Considering the tremendous changes in prospect for us as a result of German re-unification, today this is truer than ever.

Converging Policies Required in Single Market More Than a Single Currency

So I have still some sympathy for the British concept of a 'competition of currencies', or perhaps it would be better to say a 'competition of policies', at least for the time being. More than a single currency, the emerging single European market needs converging policies, which are still not in place in all participating countries. The repeated references to alleged huge savings in transaction costs for the countries of a single currency area are not in the least convincing. John Major, the British Chancellor of the Exchequer, is quite right to point out that a joint monetary policy can be very much more expensive than the conceivable savings in transaction costs because, as he fears (perhaps not without reason), it may be inferior to the present system.

So, from the German standpoint, at least, a common European currency would not only bring advantages. After all, in the Deutschemark we would be sacrificing a hard currency on the European altar without knowing what we would be getting in return. Moreover, any step in the direction of a 'Communitisation' of monetary policy in Europe means by definition a loss of room for manoeuvre for the Bundesbank, which—as I think I may say without presumption—has made a major contribution to monetary stability not only in West Germany but also in Europe as a whole (especially in those countries which have pegged their currencies to the Deutschemark). The Deutschemark's role as an 'anchor currency', which has nothing to do with 'German hegemony' (as Alan Walters has claimed) but came into being by virtue of voluntary decisions by our partners, both in the EMS and outside it (e.g. in Austria), is hardly a target for criticism nowadays (unlike the situation only a few years ago); on the contrary, it is regarded as a positive contribution to monetary stability in Europe.[1] Only recently Erich Streissler referred to the Deutschemark as a 'gold currency without gold'.[2]

If, despite this unequivocal and undeniable state of affairs, the German government is prepared to negotiate on the transfer of monetary policy decision-making powers to a Community institution, this can be accounted for only in a broader political perspective, with the long-term objective of creating a political union.[3] More recently, this has been joined by the motive of re-uniting Germany under a European umbrella, so to speak.

Whether the political considerations underlying this objective are right or wrong is not the issue I want to discuss. Everybody can have his own opinion on that point. I must, however, take note that the European heads of state and government took a decision in Strasbourg in December 1989 which will have far-reaching implications. Before the end of this year an intergovernmental conference is to be convened which is to discuss, and decide on, the future road to European economic and monetary union and its institutional structure. Its aim will be to provide the legal basis for the necessary responsibilities which now rest with the national authorities to be transferred to Community bodies. Monetary policy will be most affected. The ruling EC Treaty does not provide for any Community responsibility for monetary policy, which sufficiently explains why institutional steps towards monetary integration require an amendment of the Treaty.

I continue to have substantial doubts as to whether all or any governments would really be willing to relinquish the monetary policy sovereignty of their countries and transfer it to a Community institution. Edouard Balladur, for instance, expressed himself very frankly in a newspaper article:[4] 'Let's stop dreaming. Nobody is willing to dispense with his currency' (not to mention the strong objections of the UK). But if I work on the basis of this hypothesis, which after all

---

[1] For instance, the Delors Committee Report gave, as it were, official confirmation that the 'EMS has benefited from the rôle played by the Deutschemark as an "anchor" for participants' monetary and intervention policies'.

[2] E. Streissler, 'Unsere goldlose Goldwährung', in: v.d. Schulenburg/Sinn, *Theorie der Wirtschaftspolitik*, Tübingen: 1990.

[3] Significantly enough, the proposal to create a European currency and a European central bank did not come from the Minister of Economics or Finance, let alone from the Bundesbank, but rather from the Minister for Foreign Affairs.

[4] *Die Welt*, 25 May 1990.

underlies the intergovernmental conference, one must start to wonder what a European central bank system (ECBS) would look like—an ECBS that at the least does not fall short of the *status quo* but, on the contrary, can live up to the high expectations entertained of an institution of this kind. The Committee of EC Central Bank Governors, whose Chairman I am and which can certainly be regarded as a sort of forerunner of a possible European Central Bank Council, is working on a concept of this kind which I will no doubt be able to present to the general public shortly. Without anticipating the report and without wishing to commit anybody, I think I can safely say that *the central bank governors*, who, together with a number of other experts, have already composed the Delors Committee Report at the request of the EC heads of state and government, *are of one mind on major issues.*

EC Central Bank Must Be Politically Independent

In particular, we are agreed that historical experience shows that monetary stability can best be expected of a system which is independent of political interference. This applies to the EC to an even greater extent than to nation-states because in a confederation such as the EC there is always a tendency to orientate oneself towards averages and compromises, but that is the worst possible compass for monetary policy. Only an independent institution is in a position to resist the recurring wishes of politicians to prescribe monetary policy targets which are often inconsistent with the objective of stability, such as the stabilisation of exchange rates or the promotion of growth and employment or the balancing of regional disequilibria.

If only for practical reasons, a modern, efficient central bank system must be independent of the instructions and pressures of national governments and European institutions. Protracted consultation and concertation are inconsistent with the requirements of the financial markets, which require fast and flexible reactions by the central bank.

What is more important, however, is that only an independent central bank is in a position to pursue a monetary policy geared to longer-term requirements.[5] We know that an increase or decrease in

---

[5] Alan Greenspan, in a speech before the US Subcommittee on Domestic Monetary Policy on 25 October 1989: '. . . independence enables the central bank to resist short-term inflationary biases that might be inherent in some aspects of the political process. The Federal Reserve must take actions that, while sometimes unpopular in the short run, are in the long run in the best interests of the country'.

the money stock works through to the economy only with a substantial time-lag. Interest rate measures do not affect the money stock for several months, and price movements take even longer to react to the money stock. These delays must be taken into account when monetary policy measures are being formulated.

An independent central bank is in a better position to do so than any government, as it is not so subject to the temptation to neglect the basic requirements of anti-inflationary monetary policy for the sake of short-term effects or election tactics. William McChesney Martin (Federal Reserve Chairman, 1951-70) expressed this rather vividly when he said: 'The Fed's job is to take away the punch-bowl just when the party is getting going'.

Of course, even an independent central bank cannot alone guarantee monetary stability. The financial behaviour of the public authorities and the behaviour of management and labour must make their contribution. But the decisions of an independent central bank about the width of the 'monetary cloak' which it is prepared to provide gives an important signal for a realistic assessment of the available opportunities by all economic agents.

How Can Independence Be Guaranteed?

If it is agreed that a future European central bank system (ECBS) must be independent of governments, the Council and the Commission, the question arises as to *how this independence can be ensured*. A corresponding legal regulation which guarantees the ECBS's independence of instructions is only one element in its independence. In addition, *it requires the personal and professional independence* of the members of the governing bodies of this system; that is, of both the governors of the national central banks and the members of the supreme governing body, in other words, of the European 'Central Bank Council'.

It is important that nationality should take second place to the task with which these officials are entrusted. As there can be only one self-contained monetary policy for the Community as a whole, and not a monetary policy which takes account of the special requests of individual states and regions, the central bank governors and the members of the Board must be committed to the common task and not to the interests of individual countries or regions, and this must be clear when they cast their votes.

Above all, the instrumental independence of the system must be guaranteed—that is, its ability to fulfil its function of safeguarding monetary stability without restriction by using the necessary instruments. The instrumental independence of the ECBS must be ensured by providing it with a sufficient array of market instruments whose application is not hampered by administrative regulations and measures. These should be instruments which are linked to the markets and which use market processes to achieve their ends instead of eliminating them or falsifying them in an undesired way. It is obvious that interest rates as the price of money and credit must be of crucial importance. But this set of instruments should also include all the other tools of modern central bank policy, irrespective of whether they are being applied in the individual countries at present or not.

A system which is used only to 'co-ordinate' monetary policy but leaves the right to decide on the price and the quantity of money in circulation to the national governments and/or central banks would be 'half-baked', as Alan Walters has called the EMS. 'Co-ordination' must not be oriented towards a European inflation average or any exchange rate targets, which would amount to restricting the central banks' room for manoeuvre without providing a convincing alternative. Attempts of this nature have often been made in the last few years, as all those involved know. Such a system would be less efficient for achieving stability than the present regulatory framework of the EMS.

Independent Monetary Policy Equals Money Monopoly

Monetary policy is by its nature indivisible: an efficient central bank system must have the 'monopoly of money creation'—that is, control over the price and quantity of money. Both the Fed and the Bundesbank are to this extent centralistic, for decisions on monetary policy are taken by one body. Milton Friedman underlined this necessity in a *Financial Times* article[6] last year:

> 'A truly unified European currency would make a great deal of sense. But to achieve it requires eliminating all central banks in Europe . . . except one . . .'.

Naturally, the integration of Europe cannot be confined to monetary policy. Progress in other fields, such as the German Federal Chancellor demanded for the European Parliament, is necessary. But an independent ECBS would, in my opinion, be conceivable before the

---

[6] Milton Friedman, 'The case for floating rates', *Financial Times*, 18 December 1989.

completion of political union if the governments want it and if they are prepared to surrender the corresponding sovereignty as they have done in other, albeit less important, fields. The system would have an adequately democratic legal base if it came about by agreement between democratic governments, if the agreement were ratified by democratically elected parliaments, and if the system were provided with a clearly defined mandate.

I apologise for not being able now to go into further details on, for example, the British proposal for a 'hard ECU', but I must wind up; besides, I have expressed myself exhaustively on other occasions.[7]

But I would like to make one final remark. It will certainly be some time yet before we come to a common currency in Europe. On the way to that final step we should seek to ensure that cohesion between national economies and their currencies is strengthened.

Walter Hallstein, the first President of the EC Commission, already saw monetary policy as the touchstone for the Community. He wrote that 'monetary stability is a value of great importance, a fundamental requirement'.[8] The fact is that only when those responsible in all member-states are prepared to grant this priority to monetary stability can the project of an economic and monetary union succeed. Only then will it be possible in the foreseeable future to fix exchange rates between national currencies permanently and finally to replace national currencies by a common currency. As long as such divergences as we have today exist—differences in inflation rates between 1 and 7 per cent amongst ERM countries, for instance—it is hard to conceive how the exchange rate can be given up as an instrument of adjustment. The adjustment pressure would fall entirely on other aggregates, particularly on employment, and ever-increasing public transfer payments would become inescapable. The German monetary union provides a spectacular lesson in this respect.

Evolutionary Principles Central to European Union

The ambitious goal of an economic and monetary union in Europe certainly cannot be achieved in a revolutionary act, in a great leap

---

[7] Newspaper article, 'The vision of a European monetary area', in the *Frankfurter Allgemeine Zeitung* on 28 May 1988, and speeches in Freiburg on 7 October 1988: 'The future of the Deutsche Mark'; in Paris on 16 January 1990: 'Basic features of a European monetary order'; and in London on 2 July 1990: 'Two monetary unions— the Bundesbank's view' (reprinted as Chapter 2 of this volume, above, pp. 21-33).

[8] Walter Hallstein, *Die Europäische Gemeinschaft* ('The European Community'), Düsseldorf and Vienna, 1973, p. 133.

forward, but only in an evolutionary process which, however, should be determined by the same principles that must apply in the final stage of a European monetary order. This means that the monetary policy of the countries participating in this process must now concentrate on the task of maintaining monetary stability and preventing inflationary pressures, a task which can be pursued by central banks with the greatest chance of success.

The EMS is also illustrating this point. It too failed to stabilise until major member-states accorded monetary stability the importance which was essential to the satisfactory functioning of the system. There were no fewer than seven re-alignments up to March 1983; these are in themselves indications of instability and divergence in the terms of economic development. The decisive turnaround in the stabilisation of the EMS occurred in March 1983, when the French government radically changed its economic policy objectives. It is probably not an exaggeration to say that at that time the existence of the EMS was in the balance. Since then the 'hard core' of the EMS has come increasingly closer to the original objective, namely, to create a zone of internal and external monetary stability, which is all the more remarkable since the dollar rate was subject to extreme fluctuations in that period. The Deutschemark undoubtedly played an important rôle in this transformation, because it provided the standard of stability which every fixed exchange rate system depends on. It is in the interest not only of Germany but also of Europe as a whole that this stability 'anchor' should not be weakened, let alone abandoned, before it is ensured that something equivalent or better is to take its place.

4

PROSPECTS OF THE EUROPEAN MONETARY UNION*

Dr Karl Otto Pöhl

President, Deutsche Bundesbank

I. BRITAIN AND THE EMS

I SUPPOSE THAT in April, when you invited me to attend your conference, you already expected that the meeting would take place after Britain had joined the ERM of the EMS and that an EC-summit would announce that stage II of EMU would start in January 1994. So the topic of your conference, 'Britain and the EMS', could not have been more to the point.

The opening-up and extension of Europe is not at odds with the economic and political integration which has made such gratifying headway in the last few years. Quite the contrary: liberalisation in the east and the dissolution of the military and economic blocs have tended to stimulate interest in European co-operation among European countries which have not so far belonged to the EC.

This also applied to monetary policy co-operation, as reflected, for example, in the recent announcement by Norway that, *de facto*, that country intends to behave as if it were already a member of the EMS, and the fact that the United Kingdom has joined the EMS exchange

---

*Address by Dr Karl Otto Pöhl, President, Deutsche Bundesbank, at the Conference on 'Britain and the EMS' held in London, 9 November 1990.

rate mechanism may perhaps also be interpreted in this light. Austria has long pegged its currency to the Deutschemark—that is, it is likewise virtually a member of the European Monetary System without formally belonging to it—and I venture to forecast that other countries, too, will follow suit. This is to be welcomed, for it warrants hopes that the 'zone of monetary stability' which was intentionally to be created through the EMS will grow progressively, and also increase in international standing and weight, as is suggested by the valuation of the EMS currencies in the foreign exchange markets. From the very beginning the concept of the EMS was not that of an exclusive 'closed shop', and this should not be changed by the more far-reaching plans on Economic and Monetary Union (EMU).

Market Integration and the EMU

On the way to EMU progress has not been made only since the beginning of the so-called first stage on 1 July. The decisive impulses are coming from the integration of the market. Full freedom in the exchange of goods, services, people, money and capital—that is, the creation of the single market—has in the end been forced through markets in the context of the international division of labour.

This freedom is in fact one of the pillars of EMU. Not least, the recent liberalisation of money and capital movements by France and Italy is noteworthy in this regard. Yet a lot still has to be done before the single market becomes a reality. Let me remind you of the necessary harmonisation of indirect taxes, of industrial standards and of legal and administrative regulations, as well as of the creation of a uniform financial and banking market. Moreover, the tendency towards protectionism is still great, as we have seen recently.

Considerable progress has also been made with regard to the second pillar of EMU, the stabilisation of exchange rates within the EMS. Italy has adopted the narrow margin of fluctuation of the EMS (although it has taken more than 10 years to do so), and the UK has joined the ERM, albeit with a wide margin. But most noteworthy of all is the fact that there has been no further re-alignment in the EMS since 1987. This would not have been possible if the 'hard core' of the EMS—that is, the countries which allow their currencies to fluctuate only within the narrow margin—had not achieved a high degree of 'convergence'. This, however, is the most important precondition for the proper functioning of a fixed exchange-rate system, as was shown by the experience of Bretton Woods, as well by the history of the EMS, which in the first few years of its existence had to cope with as many as 10 re-alignments, and was on the point of collapse in March 1983.

Without the success of the EMS, current plans for Europe's further monetary integration would not be more than mere visions. The D-Mark has played a significant rôle in the EMS success story. This is generally acknowledged today, different from a few years ago, when we heard a lot of complaints about the asymmetry of the system. It is not by accident that the pound sterling, when entering the ERM, fixed its exchange rate against the D-Mark. It did so because this gives more credibility to the anti-inflationary stance in Britain. John Major, the British Chancellor of the Exchequer, recently put it this way: 'Increasingly it [i.e. the ERM] has functioned like a modern gold standard, with the D-Mark as the anchor.'

The Anchor Rôle of the D-Mark

The D-Mark grew into this anchor rôle in the EMS not by design, but by virtue of its position as the most important international currency after the dollar and owing to the inclination shown by our partners to use the D-Mark as their preferred intervention currency within the system. As a consequence, their central banks' holdings of D-Mark reserves have grown significantly over the years, a development which we resisted rather than supported but in the end could not prevent. The most important consequence of these developments is, of course, that the Bundesbank's monetary policy determines to a certain extent not only monetary conditions in Germany, but those in other European countries that peg their monetary policy to that of the Bundesbank, most obviously those countries participating in the Exchange Rate Mechanism of the EMS.

By contrast, the European Currency Unit (ECU) has never been able to assume the rôle for which it was originally designed. The ECU has had quite an impressive career, it is true, in the private financial markets, though almost exclusively in the Euro-market and in countries with relatively high rates of inflation and (until recently) foreign exchange controls. On the other hand, its monetary policy importance and its contribution to the proper functioning of the EMS have remained negligible to date. Although there have been some attempts to encourage its use, the ECU is of very little significance today as a reserve and intervention instrument among central banks.

Some of you may feel that as a result the ECU has not been given a proper chance to play its rôle at the centre of the system. But, in that case, the EMS would have been anchored to a basket unit which represents the average of members' inflation rates rather than that of the best performer. This is why the central banks—contrary to their original intentions—rejected an ECU-based intervention system from the outset, and opted for the parity grid.

That was the correct choice, as the history of the EMS has shown. It avoided placing responsibility for intervention or monetary policy adjustment on the central bank whose currency deviated from the average, regardless of the type and causes of the deviation. It would have forced better-than-average performers to accept a less rigorous monetary policy. In all probability this would have caused average inflation rates to rise, making it easier for the bad performers to continue with their easy monetary policy. So it is no surprise that the ECU's rôle in the EMS has remained marginal because, as a basket, and lacking a central bank with full responsibility for it, it could not be expected to assume a central rôle.

II. FUTURE ROLE FOR THE ECU IN EMU?

Can the ECU play a more significant rôle in the development of EMU in future? Some advocates of a European currency believe that the existing ECU can be gradually developed to perform this function. Proponents of this strategy see this as the easiest and most elegant route towards monetary unification in Europe. The ECU would simply crowd out national currencies over time, one after the other. The Delors Committee—that is to say, the 12 EC central bank governors—adopted a very clear position in this respect. It called for the removal of all impediments to the private use of the ECU. But it also firmly rejected the idea of transforming the existing basket ECU into a 'parallel currency', which would circulate all over the Community alongside national currencies. The Delors Committee did not succumb to the charms of this approach for two main reasons. It stated:

'Firstly, an additional source of money creation without a precise linkage to economic activity could jeopardise price stability. Secondly, the addition of a new currency, with its own independent monetary implications, would further complicate the already difficult effort of co-ordinating different national monetary policies.'

The British 'Hard ECU' Plan

The British Government's recently launched 'hard ECU' plan sought to avoid the shortcomings of the basket ECU. Essentially, three new elements would be brought into the European Monetary System:

(1) a 13th currency in the form of the hard ECU;

(2) new terms and conditions for the settlement of balances (in the form of a 'repurchase obligation' for the national currency by the issuing central bank); and

(3) a European Monetary Fund.

As things stand today, it cannot be said whether this would amount more to a modification of existing rules or to a substantial further development of the system. In both cases there are certainly chances of a stronger stability orientation of the system as a whole, and also of greater convergence. However, quite a number of considerable problems must likewise be taken into account. Could the 'hard ECU' crowd out national currencies in its money functions as means of payment, unit of account and store of value? What would be the consequences for the monetary policy of national central banks and for the functioning of the EMS, etc.? I cannot go into these details on this occasion.

The main problem, in my view, is which rôle the European Monetary Fund could assume and which conclusions are to be drawn therefrom for its institutional structure. As long as the Fund acts as a pure monetary authority and virtually copies the monetary policy of the most stable country, it ultimately makes no autonomous contribution to integration. Sooner or later, however, it is to be expected that this institution will develop ideas of its own about the appropriate interest-rate level and interest-rate pattern in the Community, and about exchange-rate relationships between Community currencies. This does not necessarily depend on the widespread use of the hard ECU, but hinges ultimately on the functions of the Fund and the policies of its management.

Judging by past experience, it cannot be ruled out that the Fund will be the body in which 'peer pressure' is exerted. And in that case past experience suggests that the objective of stabilising exchange rates will be preferred to that of monetary stability. 'Interest-rate leadership' in the EMS, in the direction of an increase in interest rates, is held by the Fund anyway, but it is uncertain whether, as a Community institution, it will be able to exert any pressure towards an interest-rate reduction on stability-conscious countries over the longer term. Conflicts over these questions are by no means ruled out, and the 'indivisibility of monetary policy' is not assured. If in the extreme case an 'acid test' between the ECU and the strongest national currency is to be avoided, 'compromises' in monetary policy are preprogrammed. But this is the worst possible recipe for monetary policy.

It is these imponderables, in particular, which would require a clear-cut and stability-enhancing organisation of the Fund. The appropriate criteria—commitment to the goal of monetary stability, independence, distribution of voting powers, and so on—need not be spelled out here. It is obvious, however, that the regulations must not be any softer than those proposed for the European central bank system in the Delors Committee Report. The parallel currency strategy, at any rate, offers no advantages over the Delors version on the question of the necessary institutional agreements, but it has the disadvantage that an indeterminate area of monetary policy responsibilities might emerge.

For all these reasons, the British 'hard ECU' proposal has met with little support so far. The Monetary Committee of the EC, which is composed of representatives of the finance ministers and central bank governors of the EC, has rejected the proposal by a large majority. This does not mean that it does not contain some positive features. In particular, we endorse the idea of a 'hardening' of the ECU, which might be achieved by dispensing with basket revisions in future and by not devaluing the ECU in future re-alignments. This might increase the attractiveness of the ECU for central banks, too. On the other hand, for the reasons I have mentioned, we are unable to support the proposal to create a new monetary institution because this could lead to the establishment of a grey area in monetary policy. But responsibility for monetary policy decisions is indivisible.

III. EUROPEAN CENTRAL BANK WITH SUPRANATIONAL POWERS

This can be achieved only if the decision-making power in the field of monetary policy were to be transferred to a supranational institution which ensured a common, consistent monetary policy. After a transitional period with irreversibly fixed exchange rates it could be empowered to issue a single currency. This single currency could be called ECU but—as was said already in the Delors Committee Report— it will be different from the basket ECU; in other words, it has to be a currency *sui generis*. As Milton Friedman said:

'[A] truly unified currency would make a great deal of sense. But to achieve it requires eliminating all central banks in Europe ... except one ...'.

The legal preconditions for the transfer of decision-making powers to a European central bank (ECB) are to be created at the inter-governmental conference which is due to start in Rome in December. The Committee of EC Central Bank Governors, which I have the honour to chair, will shortly be submitting the draft statute of a European central bank, which in my view should be an integral part of the envisaged amendment of the EEC Treaty. The public discussion on the basic principles of the European Central Banking System has led to a high level of agreement not only among central bankers but also among governments.

In particular, there is thus general agreement that price stability has to be the most important task of monetary policy. This actually sounds somewhat trivial, but it certainly cannot be taken for granted. The temptation to subordinate central bank policy to other goals—in particular, to exchange-rate stability—is often strong.

The conflict between 'domestic' and 'external' stability is woven into the fabric of German monetary policy like a scarlet thread: the transition about the revaluation of the D-Mark in 1968, the change to floating exchange rates in 1973, the establishment of the European Monetary System (EMS) in 1979, as well as the events in October 1987, are all milestones in the course of this conflict. In my view, it would therefore be desirable to embody in the statute of an ECB a clause to the effect that domestic stability must have priority over exchange-rate stability.

The successful pursuit of a policy of keeping prices stable is most to be expected of an independent central bank. This is so in the United States,[1] and is even more necessary for a Community institution. Members of the European Central Bank Council who are bound by instructions from their governments would represent national interests. Therefore the principle of 'one man, one vote' in this body can be implemented only if the members of the European Central Bank Council are really independent, not only in their capacity as

---

[1] '... independence enables the central bank to resist short-term inflationary biases that might be inherent in some aspects of the political process. The Federal Reserve must take actions that, while sometimes unpopular in the short run, are in the long run in the best interest of the country'. (Alan Greenspan, Chairman of the US Federal Reserve Board, in a speech to the Subcommittee on Domestic Monetary Policy, on 25 October 1989.)

council members but in their domestic functions as well. Basically, this is generally acknowledged, but it will require changes in national law in some countries to implement this principle. The democratic author-isation of an independent European Central Banking System derives from the fact that the Treaty on which it is based has been negotiated among democratically elected governments and ratified by all the national parliaments of the countries involved. Moreover, the members of the European Central Bank Council (Board) should be appointed by the European Council.

The Indivisibility of Monetary Policy

The functioning of European monetary policy requires a clear division of responsibilities between the European Central Bank, on the one hand, and the national central banks, on the other; they form the two tiers of the European Central Banking System. Although the under-lying principle is that of subsidiarity, this principle cannot be applied to monetary policy. Monetary policy decisions can be taken only by a single entity. Even under a federative system, *monetary policy must remain indivisible*: the 'monopoly of money creation' must be retained. In the European Central Banking System, therefore, it will not be possible for the national central banks to have any autonomous monetary policy powers of their own: they will only be the operational arm of the European Central Bank.

Even an independent European Central Banking System cannot guarantee price stability alone, as monetary policy does not operate in a vacuum but rather has close links to other fields. Monetary policy must in particular not be obstructed by fiscal policy. The close correlation between monetary policy and fiscal policy is entrenched not least by the temptation to finance budget deficits, allegedly without pain, via the central bank. But monetary financing of budget deficits is something that cannot be allowed. It would probably be in the interests of all the countries involved if binding budget rules were laid down and if the Community institutions were given the option of imposing sanctions if these rules were contravened. If one is realistic, one cannot expect the market to enforce the necessary degree of budgetary discipline.

This is a rough outline of the concept of a European Central Bank Constitution which will hopefully be submitted soon to the inter-government conference in the form of a detailed draft statute by the Committee of EC Central Bank Governors. In my opinion, that text should be an integral part of the EEC Treaty so that the goal envisaged is completely clear in every detail.

IV. STAGE TWO OF EMU

Clarity about the goal is absolutely essential before we can dare to go over to the so-called 'stage two'. The Heads of State and Government of the EC have already fixed a date and, gratifyingly, also the conditions which must be fulfilled for its inception. So far, however, the contents of stage two are not clear. Above all, I think it is unclear which functions the 'new Community institution' is to have which is to be established with the inception of stage two according to the 'Conclusions of the Presidency'. In the Rome Communiqué it says that, in particular, it will make it possible:

o to strengthen the co-ordination of monetary policies;

o to develop the instruments and procedures required for the future conduct of a single monetary policy;

o to oversee the development of the ECU.

In my opinion, all this does not require a new institution, let alone an ambitiously defined ECB, as this can be done just as well in the already existing, smoothly functioning institutions. On the contrary, there is the danger that an institution which will be merely an 'empty shell' without any monetary policy functions for years will not be credible from the outset.

An only partial transfer of monetary policy functions, on the other hand, should also be ruled out. There are plenty of ideas on this, as can be seen for instance, from the Delors Report, particularly its Annex. But we shall not come to like them in future either, for monetary policy responsibility is indivisible and cannot be transferred in slices. Nor is monetary policy in any way suitable for experiments with an uncertain outcome.

Conclusion

I therefore think that the European Central Bank should not be established until it has been clearly decided which countries are prepared and able, on account of their economic performance, to fix irrevocably the exchange rates of their currencies and to transfer monetary policy responsibility to the Community. The time, too, must be set unequivocally for all. This would by no means imply a delay of the process of integration; on the contrary. It would, however, prevent the creation of a grey area of monetary policy responsibility for an indefinite period.

The intergovernmental conferences which are to start in December bear great responsibility for the future of Europe. I hope that the correct signals will be sent.

5

THE THREAT OF
'FORTRESS EUROPE'

Victoria Curzon Price

Professor of Economics,
Institut Universitaire d'Etudes Européennes,
University of Geneva

I. THE RECENT TRANSFORMATION OF
THE EUROPEAN COMMUNITY

THE EUROPEAN ECONOMIC COMMUNITY (variously known as the Common Market, the European Communities, the European Community, or now simply as 'the Community') began its metamorphosis into a more market-friendly institution in 1985. Until then it had failed to emphasise the liberal elements contained in the Treaty of Rome (the 'four freedoms'), but instead had attempted to integrate the diverse European economies according to an unworkable centralising principle, namely that harmonisation of laws, regulations, standards and sometimes even prices (in particular, agricultural prices) should be achieved *before* goods, services, people and capital be allowed to move freely from one country to another. The principle was unworkable because member-states could not often agree unanimously on a uniform standard for anything—whether on weighty matters such as corporate tax law, or trivial ones such as the definition of ice-cream. But even if they *had* been able to do anything as absurd, the end-result would not have been integration, for integration of markets can take place only as a *result* of trade—and trade occurs only as a result of *differences.*

That the law of one price should reign in a single market had led to a most amazing confusion in people's minds: if economic integration means a single price (hence uniform costs), then we must start by harmonising prices and costs, and integration will follow. However, the tendency of free markets to make prices converge in a single economic space is the result of an endless *process*, not its starting-point—the good people in Brussels were tackling the problem back-to-front.

EC's New Approach: 'Mutual Recognition', Not 'Harmonisation'

This simple point was given belated recognition by the Commission in its 1985 White Paper, which proposed to move swiftly to a Single Market by 1992 relying not on the principle of harmonisation but on that of mutual recognition. As we all know (and as the Commission itself acknowledges), this 'new approach' is based on the ruling of the European Court of Justice (ECJ) in the 1979 *Cassis-de-Dijon* case, which states that products legally produced and put on sale in one member-state must be admitted freely to the market of another member-state (Article 30), even if they do not comply with its local laws. Restrictions are only permitted if the goods constitute a threat according to the terms of Article 36. Thus the ECJ shifted the burden of proof from the private exporter to prove that his product was in conformity with the laws of the importing country, to the importing state to prove that the product was actively dangerous. From then on the floodgates of competition based on *differences* were open—though not many people noticed at the time (left to itself, the information might perhaps have seeped gradually into our collective consciousness and created a competitive 'single' market in a century or two). It is worth noting, however, that the nine judges came to this economically sound conclusion by merely interpreting the relevant articles of the Treaty of Rome—which had been there all the time, but which had not been emphasised. In other words, the market-friendly aspects of the Treaty had been suppressed for 20 years by an ambitious and perhaps arrogant bureaucracy (amply supported by their counterparts in member-states).

Exactly why the Commission, in 1985, should have altered its approach to the problem of integration is of course an interesting question in its own right, probably closely related to the utter failure of the original centralising philosophy. But once the beauty, simplicity and sheer efficiency of the *Cassis-de-Dijon* approach had been understood, the Commission abandoned the old doctrine of integration based on uniformity and adopted a new one (for itself) based on diversity. This meant adopting an inherently market-friendly approach. It also implied a wrenching admission of defeat: integration of diverse economies could not be accomplished as a political, diplomatic and bureaucratic process, with the Commission in the vanguard. It could occur only as a result of the *withdrawal* of the state and its agents, by delegating the task of integration to markets.

But it is one thing to come to this conclusion theoretically, or even as a practical expedient in order to achieve rapid results (that is, a 'single' market in seven years flat). It is quite another to live with the hidden consequences. For, as academics have been quick to spot, free trade in goods and services, free movement of people, money, capital and information, based on different institutional structures and in an increasingly mobile society, mean that *every* institution of society is subjected to the most intense competition. Some (like the acceptability or not of divorce or abortions) will have only a minor influence on factor movements. But others, like the choice between a high tax/low risk or a low tax/high risk environment, or a high regulation/low growth versus a low regulation/high growth environment will start having a noticeable effect on the mobile factors in the economy, forcing us to think far more carefully than was necessary in the past about the various trade-offs.

Two aspects of the modern industrial state seem to me to be particularly at risk in such a competitive environment: the discretionary power of governments and the monopoly power of organised labour. Will they not in the end resist this pressure and turn on the system which has generated it? Some back-sliding appears almost inevitable and is in practice already occurring.

II. IMPLEMENTING THE SINGLE MARKET PROGRAMME

In short, the question is how wholehearted the conversion to market-driven integration really is. (It was always a source of wonder that the Single Market project, based on the principle of mutual recognition, should have been initiated by M Jacques Delors, a leading socialist.) The word 'subsidiarity' is suddenly *in* in Brussels. *Never let a higher level of government undertake a task that a lower level of government could undertake as well or better.* In the hands of sensible people like the Swiss, this principle has real meaning. Bern is kept weak by cantons, which are kept weak by communes, and all are kept weak by the constant threat of referenda, which keeps the political class in a permanent state of semi-paralysis.

But what does the principle of subsidiarity mean in the hands of a Commission led by M Delors? Even a *reformed* socialist must hanker after the promotion of social progress on a Continental scale, running a Europe-wide industrial and regional policy and managing money for over 300 million people. And so it is that the Commission is working hard to get social policy into the highest level of European decision-taking spheres, namely the Community itself, has already obtained the right to manage an EC MITI, and has succeeded (against enormous odds) in getting monetary union onto the agenda.

By the same token, raw competition on the basis of mutual recognition is softened by the many directives which set 'minimum acceptable levels of risk', thus in effect protecting German DIN standards from competition from Greek or Portuguese standards which might not be deemed high enough to meet the 'minimum acceptable' level. So what the Community has done is not a 180-degree turn from centralising a maximum to centralising a minimum, but a mere 90-degree turn. Thus the 'principle of subsidiarity' is meaningless *in itself*: to make it operational, one has to agree on what is fit to be attributed to each sphere; and here opinions differ, so one is back to square one.

The trouble is, however, that since socialists have lost their intellectual foundations, and can no longer proclaim the virtues of organising society on collective and egalitarian lines, they now hi-jack terms like 'subsidiarity' from a completely different family of ideas, and make them their own—without, I fear, altering their fundamental convictions in any way. In short, although one can applaud the improvement in the European Community since 1985 (which has after all been striking), one cannot relax one's critical faculties for a second. Instead they have to be re-doubled because old concepts are now clothed in reassuring phrases like 'free markets' or 'competitive forces'. Indeed, the Left's new-found enthusiasm for 'Europe' is itself highly suspect.

III. THE LINK BETWEEN SOCIALISM AND PROTECTION

All this, you might say, has very little to do with 'The Threat of "Fortress Europe"'. Not so. Socialism *leads* to protection.[1] The link

---

[1] See, *inter alia*, Ludwig von Mises, 'The Decay of International Trade', in *The World Crisis*, Graduate Institute of International Studies, London: Longman, Green & Co.,

[*Contd. on p. 57*]

between socialism and protection is perfectly straightforward. To the extent that socialism distorts relative prices (say, of labour relative to capital, or of current consumption relative to future consumption, or of labour-intensive physical goods over skill-intensive service products) it sets up relative price structures which are not compatible with the pattern of international prices. Protection is asked for and protection is granted (textiles, agriculture, steel). Do social insurance taxes weigh heavily on corporate costs? Does another increase in the minimum wage put the whole salary structure out of line with productivity growth? The answer is protection. After all, Europeans must learn to pay for what they vote for....

Another circuit (less in vogue these days, it is true) runs via Keynesian demand-management policies: the extra demand 'spills over' into foreign markets, not only diminishing the macro-economic impact of such policies but also creating a balance-of-payments 'problem'. What, then, would be more natural than to limit the external sector to more reasonable proportions?

Finally, protection grows quite naturally out of the sheer in-efficiencies of even fairly mild forms of socialism as practised with enthusiasm in Western Europe over many years. Anthony de Jasay describes this state of affairs very aptly in a recent IEA paper as:

'... social democracy, with at its base an economy capitalist enough to work, and capable of holding up a strongly interventionist and redistributive superstructure, pushing union power, regulation, egalitarianism and welfarism, but only to the point beyond which adverse economic and social trade-offs become unaffordable, and never quite going over the brink'.[2]

This kind of political and social brinkmanship led during the 1970s and most of the 1980s to high levels of unemployment and low levels of growth, creating an economic climate in which pleas for protection and subsidisation were often made and seldom refused—a trend which Melvyn Krauss spotted back in 1978 in his book entitled *The New Protectionism: The Welfare State and International Trade*.[3]

1938; Lionel Robbins, *Economic Planning and International Order*, London: Macmillan, 1937; Wilhelm Röpke, *International Order and Economic Integration*, Dordrecht, Holland: Reidel, 1960; and, more modestly, on the same theme, Gerard Curzon and Victoria Curzon Price, 'Socialism and Protection', in *Sozialismus ende einer illusion*, Zurich: Verlag Neue Zürcher Zeitung, 1988, pp. 243-60.

[2] Anthony de Jasay, *Market Socialism: A Scrutiny—'This Square Circle'*, Occasional Paper No. 84, London: IEA, 1990, p. 14.

[3] Melvyn B. Krauss, *The New Protectionism: The Welfare State and International Trade*, New York: New York University Press, 1978.

'Approximated' Social Policy to Avoid 'Social Dumping'

So the question of whether or not the Single Market will turn into a Fortress in part hinges on whether or not the EC Commission succeeds in its current bid to introduce at Community level a strong dose of 'approximated' social policy that

> 'may not, when implemented, provide grounds for any retrogression compared with the situation currently existing in each Member State'.[4]

This, in de-coded language, means raising the level of labour legislation, regulation and administration in the less advanced members of the Community to the point where they do not constitute a threat to the *'acquis social'* in the more advanced countries. As the Commission itself expresses the problem (in the context of fixed-term employment contracts):

> 'Unless safeguards are introduced, there is a danger of seeing the development of terms of employment such as to cause problems of social dumping, or even distortions of competition, at Community level.'[5]

In other words, mutual recognition of each other's labour laws is not to be: we have to 'approximate' them in an upward direction in order to avoid 'social dumping' (i.e. competition based on differences in labour laws) and prevent its logical outcome—horror of horrors—retrogression of some of the more excessive labour-protection laws in northern Europe.

The implications of the choices before us are quite startling. If labour-protection laws are 'approximated' in an upward direction at Community level, the overall level of regulation will rise, costs will increase, the southern European countries will grow more slowly, and large sections of the economy will find it increasingly difficult to compete internationally. Growth will fall, protectionism increase. If labour-protection laws are left to member-states to determine in a framework of mutual recognition of differences and competing jurisdictions, the overall level of regulation will fall, costs will decrease, the northern European countries will rid themselves (voluntarily) of some of their wilder and costlier labour laws, and the southern

---

[4] Commission of the European Communities, *Community Charter of the Fundamental Social Rights of Workers*, Luxembourg: CEC, 1990, Preamble.

[5] 'Communication from the Commission concerning its action programme relating to the implementation of the Community Charter of Basic Social Rights for Workers', COM (89) 568 final, Brussels, 29 November 1989, p. 16.

European countries will grow rapidly. Community growth rates will be substantial, freer-trade policies relatively easy to implement. . . . The ultimate irony, of course, is that it is only this second path which will permit firms in northern Europe to pay high wages and bear heavy social costs, whereas the first path actually endangers the *'acquis social'* in the long run (since protectionism locks resources into low-productivity, labour-intensive activities).

IV. INDUSTRIALISTS AND THE SINGLE MARKET

The Single Market project, radical as it is, is not very much more than what was written into the Treaty of Rome in 1957. But the method is new and the time, today, is ripe. Exactly why remains, I think, a mystery. A potent mixture of heavy and growing taxes, wider and more generous social policies and subsidisation of loss-making firms at a time when two successive oil-price increases demanded a flexible and rapid response led, undoubtedly, to the 'disastrous decades' running from the mid-1960s to the mid-1980s. By 1985 governments were receptive to a radical proposal, such as the Single Market project, especially if it came from industry itself (which it did).

But it is still mysterious, because in the midst of the worst depression since the 1930s the response, in the end, was to liberalise trade on a grand scale—a very a-typical public policy response. The reason, I believe, is that industrial pressure groups were assured of 100 per cent 'mirror' reciprocity. I have argued elsewhere,[6] with Gerard Curzon, that while reciprocity has no standing in economics (protection harms mainly those who practise it, therefore a 'concession' in trade negotiations is really doing oneself a favour), it is vital for the *process* of trade liberalisation, since trade policy is the outcome of vested power interests. The latter can be persuaded that free trade offers more opportunities than threats if they can be sure that in exchange for opening up their own markets they obtain equal access to their trade partners' larger and more numerous markets. In other words, what they ask for is sector-by-sector, 'mirror' reciprocity. This assurance GATT never managed to deliver, despite its wide membership, in view of the difficulty of guaranteeing 'mirror' reciprocity in liberalisation gains falling short of 100 per cent tariff and

---

[6] Gerard Curzon and Victoria Curzon Price, 'Non-Discrimination and the Rise of "Material" Reciprocity', *The World Economy*, Vol. 12, December 1989, pp. 481-500.

non-tariff barrier cuts, where one sector might be traded off against another, where some members could avoid all obligations to liberalise their own markets and take a free ride on the most-favoured-nation clause and, finally, where a group of highly competitive developing countries were actively encouraged to do exactly this.

'Mirror' Reciprocity Guaranteed in Single Market

On the other hand, in the context of a regional economic integration scheme like the Single European Market, sector-by-sector 'mirror' reciprocity is guaranteed. Industrialists know that in exchange for opening their own protected home market, they get exactly equivalent access to their partners' markets. They may even make the mistake of thinking that they are ahead of the game if they are swapping a small-ish 'home' market for a much larger 'community' market—the mistake of course being that markets do not 'belong' to anyone, but have, in a competitive system, to be won every day. But the fact remains that in a common market, reciprocal or 'fair' conditions of competition appear to reign, thus generating support for free trade which would otherwise be astonishing.[7] It is, after all, interesting that it was the *crème de la crème* of European industry which initiated and lobbied strongly for the Single Market programme throughout the depressed economic conditions of the early 1980s.

Will they retain their enthusiasm for it once they realise that it implies increased competition on a grand scale? The question remains open, but it is worth reflecting on the fact that Philips, one of the prime movers in the 'Round Table' of European firms promoting the Single Market project back in 1985, is today having to face some of the more disagreeable implications of wider, more open markets. How much longer before they ask for (and obtain) *extra* protection from the outside world?

In short, the only way to make sure that industrialists do not have second thoughts about the wisdom of embracing market-driven economic integration on a continental scale is to provide them with a dynamically growing economy—something which the Single European Market actually has the capacity to deliver, if only one lets it.

---

[7] It helped, of course, that a hyper-efficient country like Japan was not a member of the European Community. But one day one should call the bluff of the European automobile industry, which rests its case for protection against Japanese cars on the fact that the Japanese market for European cars is 'closed' by proposing a free trade area of all trading countries. (Gerard Curzon and Victoria Curzon Price, 'Traders and Non-Traders', *The World Economy*, Vol. 9, March 1986, pp. 19-35.)

V. THE ECONOMIC PAY-OFF OF THE SINGLE MARKET

Much controversy surrounds the extent of the gains to be expected from the Single Market. The Cecchini Report[8] puts them at between 4·5 and 7·0 per cent extra GNP growth, associated with price-level reductions of between –4·5 and –6 per cent. In other words, a supply-side shift of about 11 per cent in all is anticipated, which can be taken in different combinations of growth and easing of inflationary pressures. Sceptics have argued that the elimination of numerous small barriers to trade will have a negligible effect on efficiency, that most known scale economies are already exploited,[9] and that therefore the Cecchini Report overstates the growth potential of the Single Market. Enthusiasts argue that the Cecchini Report does not take dynamic effects into account (especially economy-wide economies of scale) and that its estimates need to be multiplied by a factor of three or four.[10]

For my own part I would tend to side with the enthusiasts for two reasons: first, the non-tariff barriers due to different technical specifications are not small (one estimate has put them at 17 per cent of costs on average[11]), which suggests that fairly substantial gains from economies of scale are available. Secondly, the Single Market includes services, which hitherto have been very heavily protected, especially financial, information and communication services. Cost reductions here would have a massive supply-side impact on the entire economy, since there is not a single aspect of the economy that they do not touch in one way or another.

It is clear, however, that whatever the size of the potential gains, they would be much reduced if a strongly interventionist and redistributive European superstructure were put in place before they even have time to materialise. As argued above, industrialists' support for the whole venture would quickly evaporate. A further protectionist twist would be hard to avoid, since the currently fashionable corporate strategy for coping with 1992 takes the form of mergers and acquisitions—creating larger units in order to capture economies of

---

[8] Summary to be found in EC Commission, 'The Economics of 1992', *European Economy*, No. 35, 1988.

[9] See, for example, Paul Geroski, 'The Choice between Diversity and Scale', in John Kay (ed.), *1992: Myths and Realities*, London: London Business School, 1988.

[10] Richard Baldwin, 'The growth effects of 1992', *Economic Policy*, October 1989, pp. 248-81.

[11] Booz-Allen & Hamilton, *The Cost of Europe's Fragmented Market*, London, 1986.

scale. However, in a world of fewer but larger firms, it is vital to keep markets contestable via imports and foreign direct investment. Otherwise the scale economies will soon be internalised by the industry itself and dissipated in X-inefficiencies. The current scale of acquisitions, mergers and joint ventures in anticipation of 1992 suggests that this is a very real possibility: without open markets, competition (and therefore efficiency) within the Single Market might even diminish. Worse, once started, the spiral would be very difficult to stop, since protectionism flourishes in depressed economic conditions.

In short, a seemingly minor policy mistake at this stage in the Single Market process could easily end in disaster.

What are the chances? The next section will discuss the most obvious starting-point of such a vicious circle—the European social charter. According to some, adding a 'social dimension' is necessary in order to ease the restructuring of the European economy as a result of the Single Market (in short, to help us cope with 10,000 job losses at Philips). According to others, reinforcing social policies is what gives rise to the dismissals in the first place.

VI. THE PRESSURE FOR A 'SOCIAL DIMENSION' TO THE SINGLE EUROPEAN MARKET

After a decade of supply-oriented policies in the United States, the United Kingdom and a handful of other countries, resulting in unprecedented growth but accompanied by a number of untidy side-effects (a combination of politics and human error), it seems to me that electorates are just about ready for a good dose of income redistribution and Welfare Statism. The plight of the homeless, the sorry state of public services, the idea that the rich have got richer and the poor, poorer—all seem to point in the same direction. The problem is that the bad economic experience of the 'disastrous decades' is associated, in the mind of the public, with the two oil-price increases and not (as it should be) with the depradations of income redistribution and the Welfare State.

So we may have to go through another cycle before the lesson is well and truly learned. One can be philosophical about this process, taking comfort in the Hayekian idea of the discovery of appropriate social institutions by trial and error, but the timing could not be worse as far as the Single European Market is concerned. For the latter is reaching maturity just as respect for markets and disillusionment with the Welfare State are (after 10 years) becoming a spent force, leaving the political turf free for yet another crack at social democracy, this time on a truly massive scale.

The 'social dimension' of the Single Market project has been present from the start—the only question being exactly how much emphasis it would be given. Thus, the White Paper (1985) states:

> 'As far as social aspects are concerned, the Commission will pursue the dialogue with governments and social partners to ensure that the opportunities afforded by completion of the Internal Market will be accompanied by appropriate measures aimed at fulfilling the Community's employment and social security objectives.'[12]

The Single European Act (SEA, Luxembourg, 1986), signed and ratified by all 12 members of the European Community, reiterates these concerns. On the one hand, it reconfirms the idea of a single market based on free competition:

> 'The internal market shall comprise an area without internal frontiers in which the free movement of goods, persons, services and capital is ensured in accordance with the provisions of this Treaty',

and

> 'The Community shall adopt measures with the aim of progressively establishing the internal market over a period expiring on 31 December 1992 ...' (SEA, Art. 8A).

On the other hand, the SEA qualifies this pro-market stance with the following commitment:

> 'Member States shall pay particular attention to encouraging improvements, especially in the working environment, as regards the health and safety of workers, and shall set as their objective the harmonisation of conditions in this area, while maintaining the improvements made' (SEA, Art. 118A, para. 1).

The essential question is whether directives implementing this objective are to be taken unanimously or by qualified majority. And here one can only say that the SEA is remarkably ambiguous. Article 118A, para. 2, goes on to say:

> 'In order to help achieve the objective laid down in the first paragraph [i.e.

---

[12] Commission of the European Communities, *Completing the Internal Market*, Luxembourg: CEC, 1985, p. 8.

the improvements in the working environment just referred to], the Council, acting by *a qualified majority* on a proposal from the Commission . . . shall adopt, by means of directives, minimum requirements for gradual implementation . . .' (emphasis added).

However, in an earlier part of the SEA, which deals with the re-introduction of the principle of qualified majority voting in order to 'achieve the objectives set out in Article 8A', the exceptions to this principle (i.e. those areas requiring unanimity) are clearly set out:

'Paragraph 1 shall not apply to fiscal provisions, to those relating to the free movement of persons *nor to those relating to the rights and interests of employed persons*' (SEA, Art. 100A, para. 2, emphasis added).

One day, the ECJ will have to rule on this ambiguous drafting, which of course is no accident but due to a fundamental divergence of view on just how much social policy should be decided upon (and how easily) at Community level.

Differences and Battlelines

In the meantime, the differences have surfaced and the battlelines have been drawn. In February 1988, the 'Delors package' reformed the Community's 'Structural Funds', thus laying an important (financial) plank in its Programme of Social and Economic Cohesion (SEA, Subsection IV) and earmarking some 60 billion Ecus for social and regional redistribution over the next five years. Jacques Delors, speaking to the European Trade Union Confederation in May 1988, promised that the impact of the Single Market would be softened by the new Structural Fund programme and would furthermore be accompanied by a 'Community Charter of the Fundamental Social Rights of Workers'. In September of the same year he repeated this promise to the British Trades Union Congress. Immediately afterwards, Mrs Thatcher took the opportunity of the opening address of the academic year at the Collège d'Europe at Bruges (to the huge embarrassment of that august institution) to warn us that Europe must not be 'ossified by endless regulation' and that she had not struggled to reduce meddlesome interventionism in the UK only to have it reimposed by Brussels.

Undeterred, the Commission proceeded to draw up its Social Charter and presented it to the meeting of the European Council in Strasbourg on 8-9 December 1989. It bears the signs of much careful drafting and re-drafting, pious references to 'the principle of subsidiarity', the 'limits' of the powers of the European Community, the 'responsibility' of member-states, and so forth. Nevertheless, it ends with the following:

> 'The European Council invites the Commission to submit as soon as possible initiatives which fall within its powers ... with a view to the adoption of legal instruments for the effective implementation ... of those rights which come within the Community's area of competence.'[13]

Exactly what are those rights which 'come within the Community's area of competence'? They are listed in the Commission's 'Action Programme' for the implementation of the Social Charter[14] and involve numerous directives in various stages of preparation. Well aware of how far it can go in 'approximating' conditions of employment, the Commission, for instance, draws the line at establishing a minimum Community wage: 'In the Commission's view, wage-setting is a matter for the Member States and the two sides of industry alone.'[15] On the other hand, it does not shrink from proposing minimum rules concerning 'the maximum duration of work, rest periods, holidays, night work, week-end work, systematic overtime'.[16] In all, some 40-odd 'new initiatives' are in preparation. Since there is no difference, from the employer's point of view, between money wages paid directly to employees, social security charges paid to the state and extra costs due to compliance with labour laws—all of which add up to the total cost of labour—there is no logical way of drawing a line somewhere down the middle, saying that money wages and social security payments should be left to member-states to determine, whilst labour laws should be approximated at Community level. The Commission's Action Plan is simply a bid to transfer a large lump of social legislation to the centre in order to protect the overblown welfare systems of northern Europe from the competition they richly deserve.

Little wonder, therefore, that at the Strasbourg meeting the Social Charter was adopted by only 11 states. ...

But the story does not end there. The Commission is arguing that these directives must be adopted by a qualified majority vote, according to Article 118A of the Treaty. The British government, on

---

[13] 'Community Charter of the Fundamental Social Rights of Workers', para. 28, referred to subsequently as the Social Charter.

[14] See note 5, above, page 58 (hereinafter referred to as the Commission's 'Action Plan').

[15] Action Plan, p. 14.   [16] Action Plan, p. 19.

the other hand, cites Article 100A as the basis of its veto power, arguing that it is not against anything listed in the Social Charter or its accompanying Action Programme, in principle, but just against the idea that Brussels should be entrusted with elaborating common or 'approximate' standards for the whole of Europe. It is a particularly good example of the difficulties of putting the principle of subsidiarity into practice.

VII. EURO-SOCIALISM: AN UNBEATABLE COALITION OF NORTH AND SOUTH?

We do not yet know the outcome of this battle, but one cannot help being struck by the fact that the United Kingdom is in a minority of one. How is it that with all the current enthusiasm for 'market forces', with the concomittant and obvious bankruptcy of socialism *as a philosophy*, and with the natural reticence of member-states to expand the powers of Brussels, the Social Charter should have got as far as it has?

We are witnessing an amazing comeback of the outdated, discredited, boring philosophy of the Redistributive Welfare State dressed up in 'European' clothes: perhaps one could call it 'Euro-Socialism'. The trouble is that having appropriated the word 'Europe', it not only benefits automatically from the widespread popularity of the idea of 'Europe', but anybody who dares object is immediately labelled 'anti-European'.[17] At a time when socialism is on the defensive from an intellectual point of view, this helps enormously in terms of practical politics. But Euro-Socialism has also found allies in unexpected quarters. Take the otherwise reasonably pro-market conservative German government. Does Mr Köhl give Mrs Thatcher a helping hand in her crusade against the 'social dimension'? Not a bit of it. He is too much of a politician for that, and knows that nothing would suit German industry and German unions better than to make sure that Greece, Spain and Portugal should raise their regulations governing working conditions to levels prevailing in the north of Europe. In the meantime, these Southern countries, which could normally be relied upon to resist having to carry such a handicap, are enthusiastically endorsing every word—partly because they have yet to go through even

---

[17] See, for example, Alan Sked, *Good Europeans?*, Occasional Paper 4, London: The Bruges Group, 1989.

the first cycle of social democracy (innocently believing that economic welfare can be made compulsory by law), and partly, no doubt, because they are convinced that the European Community will finance, one way or the other, the costs of complying.

So Mrs Thatcher is alone. But supposing Mr Kinnock (now an ardent European) were in power? How long can even Mrs Thatcher hold out against virtually universal opprobrium? For unlike the establishment of minimum acceptable standards for pressure vessels, minimum requirements with respect to paid vacations touch a universal sympathetic nerve. The Commission is on to a very good thing and its success is almost assured.

VIII. CONCLUSION

If Euro-Socialism succeeds in its take-over bid for the Single Market, it will usher in protectionism in two ways. One, directly, via the extra and well hidden costs of regulation, which will affect the whole of European industry, reduce its ability to compete with other economies bearing a lighter burden, and generally reduce its capacity to adapt, change and grow. As mentioned earlier, low growth and inflexibility produce protectionism quite naturally. The other way will operate indirectly, in that Southern Europe will require a large and growing income redistribution programme in its favour to compensate for its mysterious loss of growth. This re-arrangement of rewards will weigh heavily on the North and gradually sap its commitment to free trade. I have deliberately avoided enumerating, in this paper, the every-day evidence of mini-protectionism in the Community, introduced here and there according to this or that pressure group, and which is arguably a sort of 'normal' level of protectionist 'noise' (such as anti-dumping harassment, or the keen search for a European standard for high-definition TV). This inventory approach, though interesting, cannot tell us about past, let alone future, trends and would be incomplete without similar lists of misdemeanours committed by the United States, Japan and others. There is a sort of bed-rock level of protectionism that democratically elected governments do not seem to be able to do without—and the European Community is no exception. The Single European Market is already in the process of taking over some of the old individual protectionist measures (for instance, in automobiles), but this does not really make it a 'fortress'—yet. I have preferred instead to discuss the inner springs from which a noticeable *increase* in the level of protection might flow.

Which Way Will Europe Go?—The Optimistic View

In fact, however, the Community could go either way. One could even take an optimistic view that the 'social dimension' will remain a list of non-binding general principles, that competition within the Single Market will shake out so many old inefficiencies (including those stemming from an excess of well-intentioned but excessively costly regulation), and generate such dramatic dynamic growth (*à la* Baldwin) that the pressure for bed-rock protection might actually shrink, thus setting the European economy on a permanently higher growth-path.

This vision of a competitive Europe is tantalisingly within our grasp. It would release such energies that we could easily cope with the truly 'European' problems we need to solve, such as integrating Eastern Europe, devising a common defence strategy, coping with the environment (including paying for a huge clean-up operation all the way to Moscow and beyond), and, finally, playing a leading part in maintaining, developing and liberalising the world trade system. There is so much to be done by Europeans at the level of the Community that it would be missing a huge opportunity to let the socialists have their way. Above all, one must insist that a market-based vision of European integration is *not* being anti-European, but rather the only way to achieve, in the long run, the objectives laid forth in the Single European Act, namely for Europe

> 'to aim at speaking ever increasingly with one voice and to act with consistency and solidarity in order more effectively to protect its common interests and independence . . .'.[18]

---

[18] Preamble to the Single European Act.

6

EUROPE'S CONSTITUTIONAL DEFICIT

Frank Vibert

Deputy Director,
Institute of Economic Affairs

Summary

AS 1992 APPROACHES, large strides will have been made towards the completion of one of Britain's major priorities in Europe, the achievement of the Single Market. The inception of the Single Market will complete many of the purposes set out in the Treaty of Rome. Beyond 1992, Britain and her EC partners will wish to set new priorities. These priorities may require a rather different balance in Community structures and institutions. The techniques and institutions appropriate to push through the achievement of a Single Market may not be those appropriate to Europe post-1993, when difficult questions of monetary, social, defence and political co-operation may be on the agenda.

This chapter will therefore examine the powers of the EC Commission, and in particular its power to initiate and propose legislation; the various forms of limitations on the exercise of those powers; and the safeguards available to member-states. The chapter compares the position of member-states in the EC with that of governments and permanent institutions within other international organisations.

The chapter suggests that existing limitations on the Commission's powers—particularly its power to propose legislation—are weak.

Safeguards for a member-state placed in a minority position are fragile. There are a number of ways in which this 'democratic' or 'constitutional deficit' can be redressed. The options include institutional changes to the Commission (for example, transforming the Commission into an Executive Board, on the model of the International Monetary Fund); limitation of the power to propose legislation; and the introduction of procedural revisions into the Treaty of Rome to entrench changes in the rôle of the Commission. The chapter also examines more fundamental constitutional changes in the Treaty designed to provide an effective protection of member-states' rights and the legal rights of their citizens.

A more radical approach would be for Britain and its partners in the EC to co-operate on a more flexible basis, with different member-states grouping together as they find appropriate for different areas of co-operation. This 'multi-track' approach may provide a more effective foundation on which Europe can proceed on the diversified agenda required for co-operation in the 1990s. This approach would place more emphasis, for example, on co-operation in foreign policy, and the new defence and security arrangements that will be required in the 1990s.

I. INTRODUCTION

The scheduled completion in 1992 of the European Single Market will mark the achievement of a major aim of British policy towards the EC. Beyond this accomplishment, there will be other important objectives for Britain to pursue together with its EC partners:

o It will be necessary to maintain momentum in removing the barriers that will still remain after 1992 in the way of a free flow of capital, goods, services and labour within the Single Market.

o There will be a requirement to develop means of extending the Single Market area to include the members of the European Free Trade Association (EFTA) as well as countries in Eastern Europe pursuing market-oriented economic policies within a framework of political pluralism.

o Of fundamental importance will be the necessity for Britain and the other European members of the Atlantic Alliance to manage the re-arrangement of defence and security burdens with the United

States, within the framework of the North Atlantic Treaty Organisation (NATO).

o Other areas of co-operation between Britain and other European countries on market-oriented solutions to environmental problems, co-operation on drugs and on terrorism.

o In addition, in the light of the 'Uruguay Round' multilateral trade negotiations, scheduled to finish at the end of 1990 or shortly thereafter, the EC will need to continue to make progress on reducing its external trade barriers with the rest of the world—particularly those arising from non-tariff barriers to trade—and distortions in agricultural trade emanating from the Common Agricultural Policy (CAP).

Co-operation between EC member-states on these important post-1992 objectives would be jeopardised by serious tension in the interpretation of Community aims. The draft European Social Charter, together with Stages 2 and 3 of the Delors Committee proposals for European Monetary Union (EMU), are causes for concern. So is a lingering belief in the efficacy of large-scale public expenditure programmes in such areas as regional policy, and a remaining attachment to state-directed industrial policies affecting competition policy, external trade policy and co-operation in science and technology. In addition, the changes in Eastern Europe as well as the likely reduction in the contribution of the USA to Europe's defence call for a positive EC response.

Divergence on the objectives of European co-operation beyond 1992—beyond the completion of the Single Market—may reflect a genuine difference of opinion between Britain and its EC partners. It may, however, be the case that a major source of the difficulty stems from the EC Commission itself, a body which enjoys powers unparalleled in other international institutions. It is therefore timely to examine the functioning of the Commission and, in particular, its rôle in setting the agenda for European co-operation and in proposing policy initiatives.

II. THE POWERS OF THE COMMISSION

Compared with other international organisations, the powers of the Commission are unique in their range and scope. Four main functions can be distinguished:

o Providing a forum for consultation and review among member-states.

o Providing executive and administration services to support and implement policies decided by EC member-states.

o A regulatory and quasi-judicial function.

o The power to initiate and propose.

The Review Forum

The role of the Commission in providing a forum for 'peer' review among member-states can be illustrated in respect of the economic policies of EC members. This particular review function of the Commission essentially stems from Article 2 of the Treaty,[1] which refers to an 'harmonious development of economic activities', and Article 3(g) which refers more specifically to 'the application of procedures by which the economic policies of member-states can be co-ordinated'. This is elaborated in the Articles relating to co-operation in Economic and Monetary Policy (Part 3, II) where Article 103 states that conjunctional policies of the member-states are a matter of 'common concern'[2] and enjoins member-states 'to consult each other and the Commission'. Article 105 establishes the Monetary Committee for economic review purposes and refers also to co-operation between the central banks of member-states (through the Committee of Governors of the central banks). This mode of economic co-operation through mutual review was pioneered by the Organisation of Economic Co-operation and Development (OECD) and the International Monetary Fund (IMF) as well as, for central bankers, by the Bank for International Settlements. While views about the effectiveness of multilateral surveillance of this type have waxed and waned, it is a well-established manner of co-operation which provides the formal backdrop to the practical co-operation occurring by direct communication between central banks and ministries of finance when required.

---

[1] References to 'the Treaty' refer to the 'Treaty Establishing the European Economic Community' as amended by the Single European Act (SEA).

[2] The same language of 'common concern' is incorporated in Article 107 in respect of the exchange rate policy of each member-state.

The Executive Rôle

The powers of the Commission extend well beyond those of a consultative forum, like the OECD. This is on account of the Commission's responsibilities for the *execution and administration of EC policy* in several huge areas. Their administrative responsibilities had their origin in the implementation of the original customs union between EC member-states and in the CAP. Other areas of executive and administrative responsibility include:

o negotiating the common external trade arrangements of the community (Articles 111 and 112);

o concluding association agreements with other states including those countries associated through the Lomé Convention;

o and administering various funds, including the European Social Fund (Article 124) and the Development Fund for Associated Countries.

In its executive rôle the Commission acts much as a civil service department within a national administration. In respect of other international institutions there are analogies with the executive responsibilities of, for example, the Bretton Woods institutions (the World Bank and the IMF).

The Regulatory and Quasi-Judicial Function

The powers of the Commission extend well beyond those of the Bretton Woods institutions in respect of its *regulatory and quasi-judicial functions*. For example, it has the power to issue directives to member-states[3] on internal EC trade (Articles 13 and 33), on the Common Agricultural Policy (Article 45), and on Competition Policy (Article 90). It has the general power to bring legal action in the Court of Justice against a member-state which fails to fulfil its 'obligation under this Treaty' (Article 169), and a faster procedure is allowed in respect of Single Market obligations under Article 100(a).

The Commission has a general power to carry out investigations and, in more specific areas of the CAP, internal and external trade policy, transportation and competition policy, its powers may include the capacity to authorise, make rules, lay down provisions applicable to, and to 'take decisions'. Its quasi-judicial function to give 'a reasoned

---

[3] Directives are left to member-states to incorporate in an appropriate way into their national law.

opinion' is expressed in both a specific context (Competition Policy, Article 89) as well as more strikingly in general terms in Article 170, which states that member-states bringing an action against another member-state must first bring the issue before the Commission which then 'shall deliver a reasoned opinion'.

Initiation and Proposal

Last but not least, the Commission has the power to *propose legislation*. Throughout the Treaty from its first occurrence in Article 7 runs the formula, 'The Council may, *on a proposal from the Commission . . .*' (emphasis added). The reference to the Commission's rôle in initiating, recommending and proposing permeates the Treaty. The power is expressed in general and open-ended terms in Article 155 which states (*inter alia*):

'In order to ensure the proper functioning and development of the common market the Commission shall . . . formulate recommendations and deliver opinions on matters dealt with in this Treaty, if it expressly so provides *or if the Commission considers it necessary*' (emphasis added).

References to the rôle of the Commission in bringing proposals forward are contained over 80 times in the 248 Articles of the Treaty (excluding its annexes and protocols). The sweep of the Commission's powers raises many issues including the Commission's accountability, the extent to which its actions are subject to effective review and scrutiny, and the extent to which there is effective procedure for judicial review of its actions. They raise in particular the question as to whether it is prudent to encompass within one organisation such a wide range of functions. Especially important in view of the necessity to establish priorities for European co-operation beyond 1992 is the Commission's rôle as a proposer of policies. It is this rôle, incorporated in so many references within the Treaty, which appears to underlie many of the divergences between objectives for a market-oriented Community and proposals in which the Commission may have a vested bureaucratic interest.

III. THE CONCEPT BEHIND THE COMMISSION'S POWERS

The origins of the power of initiative of the Commission lie in its precursor, the High Authority of the European Coal and Steel Community (ECSC). The High Authority was set up with supranational ambitions and functions. Indeed the rôle of member-states acting through the Council of the ECSC was defined (in Article 26): 'to harmonise the action of the High Authority and that of the Governments', this formulation clearly reflecting the rôle, independent of governments, envisaged for the High Authority. In the case of the EC, the executive and administrative functions of the Commission have been set out with a greater degree of restriction in relation to the rôle of the Council. Nevertheless the power of initiative remains with the Commission and successive Commissions have used this power of initiative, in conjunction with other Commission powers, to insist on an independent role for the Commission *vis-à-vis* the member-states. As Roy Jenkins has recorded of one of a recurring number of instances during his Presidency of the Commission,

'the real issue was the independent position of the Commission as opposed to its subordination to member-state governments'.[4]

Lying behind this desire of the Commission to retain an independent rôle and, in particular, the power of initiative, has been a vision of a process of European integration steered by the Commission with some form of potential union at the end of the road. The Commission has seen itself as a European 'government in embryo', and Roy Jenkins has not been alone in envisaging his rôle as President of the Commission as a putative Prime Minister of Europe.

The power of initiative has been crucial for the Commission's efforts to set an agenda leading towards European union. Roy Jenkins records of his initiative on monetary union:

'as ... none of the three main governments ... was prepared to support a major Commission initiative, we ... had to be prepared to go against them and to blaze a trail'.[5]

More recently, President Delors has said that

'it is above all in exercising its right of initiative that the Commission shoulders its responsibilities. And everyone gives it credit for having defined goals and proposed ways and means of revitalising European integration. The Commission intends to retain this dynamic approach, assuming it can come up with new ideas and options'.[6]

---

[4] Roy Jenkins, *European Diary, 1977-81*, London: Collins, 1989, p. 106.
[5] *Op. cit.*, p. 135.
[6] Speech to the College of Europe—Bruges, 17 October 1989.

Whatever the attitude towards the goal of European political union, there must be a serious question as to whether the techniques of dynamic legislative initiation and regulatory control which were appropriate to introduce a Single Market, against vested interests within member-states, are appropriate to the questions of monetary, social, political and defence co-operation that may form the post-1992 agenda. Emerging concern about a 'democratic deficit' may need to be matched by concern about a 'constitutional deficit', and by fresh consideration of the institutions which may be relevant to the EC once the Single Market has largely been completed.

IV. THE LIMITS OF THE COMMISSION'S POWER

In considering existing limits on the Commission's powers, it is useful to distinguish four main sources of restraint:

○ those stemming from the Council (representing the member-states);

○ parliamentary control (whether exercised through the European Parliament or through national parliaments);

○ judicial restraints;

○ 'doctrinal' control—the attempt to define through the principle of 'subsidiarity' a demarcation between the sphere of national competence and the areas which are of transnational European concern where the Commission may have a legitimate rôle delegated to it.

The Council

The Council represents member-governments through the ministers responsible for their subject areas. Foreign Ministers have traditionally been concerned with work in progress as a whole and in preparing for the meetings of Heads of Government in the Council of Europe. The Treaty accords the Council the 'power to take decisions' (Article 145) and the same Article specifies that the Commission's powers of implementation stem from the Council—the Council shall 'confer on the Commission . . . powers for the implementation of the rules which the Council lays down'.

Over the years the Council, supported by the permanent representatives of member-governments (COREPER), have together been seen to strengthen their position *vis-à-vis* the Commission. It is significant that the procedures for co-operation on foreign policy (Title III of the Single European Act), which is an area of co-operation of more recent origin, concedes to the Commission a distinctly subordinate rôle (Article 30). The Commission is to be 'fully associated with the proceedings of Political Co-operation', but there is no mention of a Commission rôle in initiating or proposing policy and there is a separate secretariat directly responsible to the Presidency of the Council.

Nevertheless, the Council's ability to control the Commission is far from absolute. Inevitably and desirably there will be differences of opinion between member-governments on matters under consideration, *communiqués* which paper over differences or seek refuge in ambiguity,[7] and it is these differences which the Commission is able to exploit through its power to initiate and propose. In some respects the Commission's aspirations to an independent and autonomous rôle involve form rather than substance. Roy Jenkins recalls:

> '[T]here wasn't any real issue of substance ... but equally we [the Commission] strongly took the view that as an independent institution we could not just say, "Yes, Yes", to any last-minute decision of the European Council.'[8]

The Commissions's power to propose can, however, also be used to real effect to promote the Commission's own agenda and to exploit differences of opinion among member-states. Concern about the Council's power, and in particular about its responsiveness to national government considerations, has recently been made evident in President Delors's suggestion that permanent ministerial Council members should be appointed, at Deputy Prime Minister level, to secure continuity and more rapid decision-taking. The intent of this proposal is not to strengthen the Council but rather to weaken the extent to which the Council reflects the voice of member-states.

Parliamentary Limits

Parliamentary limits on the Commission are weak. Article 144 provides for the European Parliament to be able to censure the Commission (by a two-thirds majority of the votes cast by a majority of members) but the

---

[7] See, for example, the 'Solemn Declaration of Stuttgart' of 19 June 1983.

[8] *Op. cit.*, p. 189.

reality is not of a parliamentary body set to ensure that the Commission does not overstep its powers or to keep it to account. On the contrary, the Commission and the European Parliament may see each other as allies in extending the powers of each in relation both to national parliaments and to member-governments. The co-operation procedure contained in the Single European Act was designed to provide for a stronger European Parliament rôle *vis-à-vis* the Council. Yet the effect of these provisions is potentially to strengthen the hand of the Commission *vis-à-vis* the Council. Article 149 envisages that the Commission may have an independent position on an issue having a qualified majority in the Council which it is to communicate to the Parliament (Article 149, 2(b)); amendments proposed by Parliament are to be re-examined by the Commission and proposals re-examined by the Commission and presented to the Council may only be amended by the Council if it acts with unanimity. The Commission thus gains a valuable 'middleman' rôle which accompanies its right in Article 155 to participate in 'the shaping of measures' by the European Parliament and the right of Commission members to attend all meetings of the European Parliament and to be heard 'at their request' (Article 140). Rather than the European Parliament acting to check the Commission, the reality is the potential use of the Parliament by the Commission as an instrument in order to assert its independent policy-making rôle.

Parliamentary review of the Commission by national parliaments also offers little effective mechanism for scrutiny. In the case of Britain, the relevant committees of the House of Commons and House of Lords have no direct relationship with the Commission and conduct their scrutiny function primarily through government evidence and within circumscribed terms of reference.

Judicial Review

Judicial restraints on the Commission rest essentially with the European Court of Justice. They stem from Article 4 which states that 'Each institution shall act within the limits of the powers conferred upon it by this Treaty'. According to some eminent authorities,[9] this provides the Court with a foundation to reject acts of the Commission on a basis broadly equivalent to the doctrine, familiar in English law, of

---

[9] D. Lasok and J. W. Bridge, *Law & Institutions of the European Communities*, London: Butterworths, 4th edn., 1987.

'ultra vires'. Lack of competence, together with other grounds for the Court to review the legality of the acts of the Commission, are reflected in Article 173.

It must, however, be questioned whether Articles 4 and 173 do in practice provide for effective judicial restraints on the Commission. First, absent from the Treaty is any sense of 'checks and balances' whereby the Court of Justice would have a clear and, if necessary, adversarial responsibility to keep the executive and legislative branches of government not only within their limits, but also from co-mingling executive, legislative and judicial powers.

Secondly, public choice theory requires examination of the self-interest of institutions.[10] An institutional self-interest of the Court of Justice and of the Commission may both lie in the same direction—in the extension of Community law and competence. As with the European Parliament, the Commission may in practice have an ally in the Court rather than an effective restraining institution.

Thirdly, the Court from its own perspective may see the Commission as its ally. Important in this respect is Article 169 empowering the Commission to bring member-states before the Court of Justice. The Court will thus see an activist Commission as important for the maintenance and extension of its own power.

Fourthly, the doctrine of 'competence' and the reach of Article 173 cannot extend to 'recommendations or opinions' but only to acts. Thus there is no judicial restraint on the Commission's power to initiate and propose in any area, *including areas outside its competence.*

Doctrinal Restraints

A final category of limit on the Commission is the doctrine of *'subsidiarity'*. Akin to a generalised demarcation between federal rights and states' rights, the doctrine attempts a similar division between matters which lie within Commission prerogatives and those matters where member-states should retain their prerogatives. The principle can be expressed as follows:

> '[T]he Commission's sphere is to carry out only those tasks which may be undertaken more effectively by the member-states acting in common rather

---

[10] See, for example, James D. Gwartney and Richard E. Wagner, 'Public Choice and the Conduct of Representative Government', in James D. Gwartney and Richard E. Wagner (eds.), *Public Choice and Constitutional Economics*, Washington DC: Cato Institute, 1988.

than separately and in respect of those tasks whose dimension or effects extend beyond national frontiers.'

Depending on how it is expressed, this theoretical divide is weak, subjective and open-ended. It is insufficient by itself and in any event not yet properly reflected in the Treaty.

This brief review of the limits on the Commission's power shows that, with the exception of the limits imposed by the Council itself, the restraints are weak. Particularly important is the absence of any restraint on the Commission's powers to initiate and propose, even in areas outside its competence. This is absent not only in the judicial restraint but also strikes at a vulnerable point in the control exercised by member-states through the Council. It is a weakness fully exploited by the Commission.

'The lesson he [Jean Monnet] taught me was always to advance along the line of least resistance provided that it led in approximately the right direction.'[11]

That 'right direction' may consist of a view about European union which is markedly more extensive than that which exists at member-state level.

It may be argued that the power of the Commission to propel member-states in directions they do not wish to go is strictly curtailed by the safeguards in the Treaty—particularly those related to voting. The nature of those safeguards is next examined.

V. SAFEGUARDS FOR MEMBER-STATES

The Unanimity Requirement

The traditional safeguard for member-states in resisting proposals and institutions of which they did not approve has been the requirement for the *unanimous approval* by member-states in most areas of decision. However, in order to implement the Single Market programme, Britain agreed to an extension of majority voting. There is now the clear likelihood that this provision for majority voting established in the Single European Act will be used in areas on initiatives of which Britain does not approve.[12]

---

[11] Roy Jenkins, *op. cit.*, p. 23.

[12] Article 100 (a) does define a unanimity requirement for fiscal provisions, provisions relating to the free movement of people and the rights and interests of employed persons. Whether these exceptions could be challenged on an alternative Treaty base remains to be seen.

This possibility arises essentially for two reasons. First, Article 100(a) which introduces majority voting for the implementation of the Single Market has been framed in broad terms without defining 'the Single Market' and, in particular, without distinguishing between the term 'Single Market' and 'Common Market'. A second and related cause for concern is that the Single Market provision for majority voting provides other member-states and, in particular, the Commission with an alternative treaty base on which to rest actions and initiatives compared with the unanimity required when the same subjects are treated in other areas of the treaty. Cases relating to the choice of treaty base are being brought before the Court of Justice, but, as mentioned earlier, the Court may tend to side with the Commission rather than with member-states in its interpretations. In short, the majority voting provision which Britain saw as a limited departure from the normal unanimity safeguard may turn out itself to become an important basis on which the Commission rests its initiatives, leaving the unanimity safeguard emasculated.

Blocking Minorities

The possibility that the majority voting provisions of the amended Treaty will be used by the Commission and/or other member-states on proposals to which Britain is opposed, is reduced to some extent as long as Britain can persuade other member-states to join it in opposition to an unwanted initiative. As Sir Geoffrey Howe stated in the debate on the Treaty amendments: 'it will be open to us to combine with other members to form a *blocking minority*'.[13] It should be noted, however, that in order to block a proposal of the Commission under the majority voting provisions of Article 148, Britain will not be able to block with the support of one other of the 'Big Four' alone. Britain will always need to be joined by at least two other member-states, including one of the Big Four. If the Commission is supported by each of the Big Four other than Britain, Britain will need to gain the support of at least 12 of the remaining 36 votes in order to block the initiative, involving the support probably of at least three of the remaining eight member-states. Given the relationships involved, it is unlikely that Britain will be able to block a Commission proposal that has the support of the Big Four other than Britain itself.

---

[13] *Hansard*, 23 April 1986.

The 'Luxembourg Compromise'

If Britain is outvoted on a Commission proposal, the 'Luxembourg Compromise' remains as a 'last resort'. Under this unwritten procedure, a member-state may insist that the issue concerned raises a matter of 'supreme national interest' and that therefore discussion should continue until unanimity has been reached or its objections removed. However, Britain's invocation of the Luxembourg Compromise may be rejected by the other member-states and, since it is nowhere incorporated in the Treaty, it is unlikely to stand if challenged before the Court of Justice. It is a 'safeguard' which rests on the goodwill of other members at the time at which it is invoked. It is significant that President Delors has referred to 'the pseudo-compromise reached at Luxembourg' and suggested that

> '... the old "inequality-unanimity-immobility" triangle has been replaced by a new "equality-majority-dynamism" triangle, the key to success. We will need to draw conclusions from this experiment when the time comes to make further improvements to our institutional apparatus'.[14]

Derogation

A final line of defence for Britain in opposing proposals or acts of the Commission to which it is opposed would be through a *derogation* procedure. However, the instances when a member-state can formally opt out of a Community requirement are extremely limited (see, for example, Article 73(2) in relation to capital controls). They are in any event subject to Commission challenge or authorisation. Essentially, under present treaty arrangements, a member-state wishing to opt out of arrangements approved under majority voting provisions which it had failed to block, would have to resort to a position of defiance— which, in the final analysis, would mean defiance of other member-states, the Commission and the Court of Justice.

Thus, in summary, not only are the limits weak on the sweeping range of Commission powers, but the safeguards for Britain in resisting Commission proposals to which it objects are also fragile. While Britain can, and should, attempt to gain the support of other member-states for its views about priorities beyond 1992, the Commission's powers to initiate and propose its own agenda can create a major source of tension between member-states.

---

[14] Speech to the College of Europe—Bruges, 17 October 1989.

Before considering the various potential approaches towards overcoming these problems, it is useful to look further at the way in which certain other international organisations structure their institutions.

VI. INTERNATIONAL INSTITUTIONAL COMPARISONS

Examination of the EC Commission in relation to the secretariats of other international institutions is illuminated by points of comparison with the Bretton Woods institutions (the World Bank and the International Monetary Fund) since they, too, have important executive responsibilities in their spheres of activity; at the same time they possess considerable operational freedom.

Comparison with Senior Management of IMF and World Bank

A first point of comparison is in respect of the relationship between the senior management of the Bretton Woods institutions, equating to the EC Commission, and the governments of member-states (in the case of the World Bank, the shareholders). Since the early days of both institutions, senior management of the Bretton Woods institutions have possessed considerable executive discretion. In broad terms, they conceive their rôle as to act for the membership as a whole. Only rarely do they appear beholden to the particular member-state to which they owe their appointment or selection and their credibility is weakened when they do so. Yet this convention does not mean that the management bodies of these international organisations operate as embryonic global governing bodies, independent of their shareholder member-states. In the World Bank and IMF, management cannot embark on an adversarial relationship with any member-state, let alone a major one. They cannot indulge in public debates with major shareholders or in sustained public criticism of them. They act as international civil servants, not as rival authorities. Recently some have been concerned that the EC Commission has acted otherwise, in particular in its approach to the 'competing currencies' proposals advanced by the UK Government.[15]

A second point of comparison arises in respect of the Executive Boards of the Bretton Woods institutions. Appointed by member-

---

[15] See, for example, the *Daily Telegraph* (3 November 1989), quoting unnamed 'senior sources in the Commission' as saying that the competing currencies approach would be treated 'as little more than a joke'.

governments mainly from the ranks of senior civil servants and, in most cases, returning to civil service or related appointments after spells on the Executive Boards of usually 2-3 years, Executive Board members do not normally involve themselves in the day-to-day running or operations of either institution. However, they act as the eyes and ears of member-governments to whom they have a reporting/ representative relationship. Equally important, they act as a sounding board of the views of member-states for senior officials. This means that potential areas of dispute can often be headed off and not have to come to formal vote. It means that policy issues are identified early and are discussed in the Executive Boards before being settled at a political level if they are of sufficient importance.

In the case of the EC Commission, the tendency of the Commission to act independently of member-states has meant that a parallel machinery of government representatives (COREPER) has had to play a part alongside the Commission. The crucial functions of COREPER are not reflected in that part of the Treaty of Rome dealing with community institutions, except by summary reference in Article 151 to the provisions of the Merger Treaty. The issue is whether a more harmonious running of executive functions in the community might not be achieved by having an Executive Board of senior civil servants at the top of the Commission, rather than Commissioners drawn from the ranks of politicians and with a perception and practice of their rôle as an embryonic federal government.

A third point of comparison arises in respect of the rôle of national parliaments in ultimate control over the financial resources of the Bretton Woods institutions. Under the arrangements that have existed to date, both Bretton Woods institutions require their capital resources to be voted by the parliaments of member-states, usually at three to five-year intervals. While rarely used for scrutiny purposes by national legislatures (with the exception of the US Congress), nevertheless, in formal terms these occasions provided opportunities for national legislatures to review any aspect of the institutions. By contrast, in the case of the EC Commission, the occasion afforded for financial review arises not for the national parliaments of national states but through the annual budget review process conducted by the European Parliament.

Weakness of Financial Control in EC

The effectiveness of this procedure can be questioned from a number of perspectives. *First*, as already mentioned, the European Parliament and the Commission may well see themselves as allies, with a common interest in expansionary programmes and mutual recognition and validation of each institution's competence. *Secondly*, this review process means that there is *no* effective link between Euro-parliamentary review of the expenditure implications of community programmes, and taxation responsibilities which remain with national legislatures. *Thirdly*, the absence of effective links between national parliaments and the European Parliament, together with a lack of connection between the composition of the European Parliament and the governments of member-states, means that the review process is disembodied from national procedures for scrutiny and accountability. *Finally*, the European Parliament is less likely to represent opinion on European programmes as much as the state of voter satisfaction or dissatisfaction with their national governments at the time when European elections take place.

The issue is whether it would be desirable to provide for an effective review of Commission activities by the parliaments of member-states. Tradition would suggest that effective review is more likely if connected with the provision of finance for the Commission and would be weakened to the extent that the Community is provided with its 'own resources'.

A final point of comparison arises in respect of policy initiatives relating to the activities and responsibilities of the Bretton Woods institutions. While proposals may emanate from the staff and managements of each institution, the combination of the management/shareholder relationship mentioned earlier, with the rôle of the Executive Boards, together with the machinery at political level of the Interim and Development Committees, means a policy process more tightly managed by member-states.

Thus, while the powers of the Commission are much more sweeping in their scope than, say, the powers of the Bretton Woods institutions, these points of comparison suggest that procedures for ensuring the Commission's accountability to member-governments could usefully borrow from analogous practices in other international organisations.

VII. OPTIONS

Britain and its fellow member-states in the EC have an important responsibility in setting priorities for co-operation beyond 1992. This process could be subverted by the pursuit of an independent agenda by the Commission. Existing constitutional and institutional limits on the Commission are weak, and its powers notably larger than those applicable to the secretariats of other international organisations. In the event that priorities are set in directions which Britain or any other member-state does not agree with, the safeguards for such member-states are fragile. The risks arising from the pursuit of divergent priorities have been heightened by the extension of majority voting under the Single European Act.

In looking at ways in which member-states can establish a more orderly process for setting priorities beyond the Single Market objective, and in ways which will provide for greater safeguards for dissenting members, there are five key options:

o to modify the Commission as an institution;

o to refocus the powers of the Commission;

o to introduce procedural changes into the Treaty of Rome;

o to make constitutional amendments to the Treaty of Rome;

o to explore the possibilities of co-operation in Europe on a flexible, 'multi-track' basis.

Each of these options is outlined below.

Modifying the Commission as an Institution

One option is to *define more narrowly the functions of the EC Commission* by replacing political Commissioners by an Executive Board, clearly answerable to member-governments, and operating as civil servants. In the area of initiation and proposal a Commission in such a form would function as a secretariat to facilitate the work of COREPER and the Council. The primacy of the Council, representing ministers of elected national governments, would be emphasised and the rôle of COREPER would be made explicit. The institutional relationships in all areas of the Commission's work would parallel those set out recently in the Single European Act for co-operation in the sphere of foreign policy.

Refocussing the Powers of the Commission

The most fundamental change in the powers of the Commission would be to *modify its rôle to initiate and propose*. While in practice some policy proposals might still emanate from the staff and management of the Commission, the initiation of policy would be the clear responsibility of the Council supported by COREPER. The work of the Commission would centre around its executive and regulatory rôle. In order to focus on these regulatory functions, responsibilities for other kinds of initiative, such as spending programmes (for example, the development aid funds), should probably be transferred to specialised agencies, such as the European Investment Bank.

It would also need to be examined whether the Commission's powers of regulatory control should themselves be defined more narrowly. The power to investigate and prosecute, as well as to authorise, give reasoned opinions, and decide may be too comprehensive.

Procedural Revisions in the Treaty

Changes as outlined above would involve *revisions* to the Treaty. With the principal exception of replacing Commissioners with an Executive Board answerable to member-governments, such changes concern processes. There may, however, be a need for a broader review of the Treaty from a procedural perspective at the time of the next revision. At such an opportunity the more than 80 instances referring to the Commission's rôle in initiating proposals would be possible candidates for reconsideration, as well as a recasting of Article 155 on the general rôle of the Commission.

Changing the Constitutional Provisions of the Treaty

Because Britain does not itself have a written constitution, there is perhaps a tendency to ignore the written document. Yet viewed as a constitution the Treaty is gravely defective. There is no enumeration of the rights and prerogatives of member-states, or attempt in even general terms to incorporate such important principles as 'subsidiarity' which might aim to demarcate responsibilities. There is no attempt to provide for checks and balances between executive, legislative and judicial functions of the type which would be regarded as essential for the constitution of a modern state. Yet such separations of power may be necessary in order to transform the ill-defined notion of Commission 'competence' into an effective doctrine of *'ultra vires'*. The position of a member-state that finds itself in a minority is not adequately safeguarded and there is an absence of meaningful procedures allowing, for example, for derogation or opting out. Ambiguities in the Treaty, such as the reference in the preamble to

European 'union' which at one end of the interpretative scale may mean 'co-operation' between member-states and, at the other, the concept of a unitary state, constitute an increasingly grave problem. They lay the basis for activist interpretations of the Treaty provisions rather than judicial limits.

The democratic rights and civil liberties of individuals are mentioned only in passing. The Treaty is showing its age: its framers were more concerned with providing a supranational platform for benevolent bureaucrats than a framework and processes for the exercise of political choice by the citizens of member-states. The absence of Treaty references to national parliaments reflects a desire of the Treaty-framers to bypass national procedures rather than to use them as a building block for co-operation between democracies.

Britain has opposed Treaty revision in the past because of the risk that once basic constitutional questions are opened it will be impossible to reach agreement, and as a result progress in areas for practical co-operation will be impeded. The Commission and certain member-states are now proposing Treaty revision in connection with Economic and Monetary Union (EMU). Britain should make clear that if Treaty revision is to be considered, it should include the limited procedural changes related to limiting the Commission's place in Community processes and that any attempts to introduce fundamental changes or new Community institutions (such as a European Central Bank) should be preceded by full-fledged constitutional review.

'Multi-Track' Europe

A fifth option is to revive the idea of a 'flexible' Europe of the sort suggested by the Prime Minister in her paper tabled for the June 1983 Stuttgart Summit. The idea that different member-states in Europe might co-operate in flexible groupings in different areas of concern has been opposed in the past. Nevertheless, it has considerable merit in examining priorities beyond 1992. Extending the Single Market should not necessarily involve EFTA countries in accepting the Common Agricultural Policy, for example. Nor is it clearly evident that, once the Single Market is secured, it will remain necessary to extend use of majority voting with its temptations to political 'dynamism' for the Commission.

At the other end of the spectrum, co-operation between France and Britain on defence arrangements will need to be particularly close in the light of the growing importance of the Anglo-French nuclear capability, whereas 'neutral' countries, such as Austria, Ireland, Sweden and, possibly, new East European associates, cannot be easily included in co-operation on defence arrangements. The rôle of such neutral countries in foreign policy co-operation must also be questionable. The need to co-operate more closely on combatting terrorism should not be held up for those countries that are willing to co-operate by those that are reluctant. It is also possible that some countries would wish to proceed with EMU while others did not, and stayed out of the ensuing arrangements.

These various options are not mutually exclusive. It would be possible for co-operation to proceed on different objectives for different countries at the same time as proceeding on Treaty revisions and on refocussing the powers of the Commission. If, however, Treaty revisions cannot be negotiated and if achieving agreement between Britain and its partners on priorities post-1992 remains hampered by the Commission's power to propose its own agenda, then a multi-track Europe is the natural and obvious outcome.

VIII. CONCLUSIONS

Co-operation in Europe post-1992 will involve continuing efforts to make the Single Market a permanent reality and to extend its boundaries to embrace other European countries, as well as a much greater focus on foreign policy and defence and security arrangements. The EC Commission is not well-equipped to deal with this diversified agenda. There is real concern that it pursues its own agenda in favour of new areas of interventionism, new institutions and expanded public expenditure programmes. This deflects attention from more funda-mental priorities and complicates the process for achieving agreement on priorities between Britain and its EC partners. The idea of pursuing more flexible forms of co-operation in Europe, with different groupings of countries coming together on different priorities, could well be the most appropriate way to handle a diversified agenda in the 1990s. But, in addition to a 'multi-track' vision of co-operation, it will be necessary to re-examine Europe's constitution as presently set out in the Treaty of Rome and amended by the Single European Act. Viewed as a constitutional document it is seriously deficient. Viewed as enshrining a process for co-operation between member-states it has major shortcomings.

Tackling either the procedural deficiencies or the more fundamental constitutional flaws will, on either course, involve a redefinition of the range of powers of the Commission and changes to the Commission as an institution. The least of these changes would entail removal of the Commission's powers to initiate and propose. A more appropriate model for the rôle of the Commission is contained in the procedures for co-operation on foreign policy in the Single European Act. Revision of the Treaty is now being advocated by proponents of EMU. It is not clear that a 'multi-track' Europe requires Treaty revision at this point. If, however, Treaty revision is to be tabled, in whatever context, Britain could make it a condition of Treaty review that changes in the rôle of the Commission should be examined, and will be on Britain's own agenda.

Rooted in the experiences of the 1930s and 1940s, the founders of the institutions of the EC looked to unelected officials to play a rôle above that of member-governments and to entrust these officials to unfold a superior vision of where priorities lay. This deeply undemocratic concept is an inappropriate basis for co-operation between European democratic states in the 1990s and beyond.*

---

*This chapter is a revised version of the paper first published as *IEA Inquiry* No. 13 in November 1989.

APPENDIX

An Expansionist Interpretation of Treaty Powers

This Appendix notes some instances in which the Commission has taken a dynamic or expansionist interpretation of its Treaty powers.

Thrust of the Treaty of Rome

The Treaty of Rome does not require the Commission to harmonise every law in sight. It permits 'the approximation of laws of Member-states *to the extent required for the proper functioning of the common market*'.[1]

The Single European Act does not replace the Treaty of Rome—it complements it with a particular programme to establish the *internal market* by 31 December 1992. The internal market is

> 'an area without internal frontiers in which the free movement of goods, persons, services and capital is ensured in accordance with the provisions of [the Treaty of Rome]'.[2]

The thrust of the combined document is liberal and deregulatory—especially in such areas as:

○ Elimination of customs duties (Articles 12-17);

○ Setting up of common customs tariff (Articles 18-29);

○ Elimination of quantitative restrictions between member-states (Articles 30-37);

○ Free movement of persons, services and capital (Articles 48-73);

○ Transport (Articles 74-84);

○ Rules against distortion of competition (Articles 85-94).

Yet the Commission has used such measures to foster harmonisation well beyond 'the extent required for the proper functioning of the common market'.

Article 54

For example, even before the signing of the SEA, it used Article 54(3)(g) of the Treaty to promote two-tier boards or works councils for

---

[1] Article 3—emphasis added.

[2] Article 8 (a), introduced into the Treaty by the SEA.

all large community companies. Yet this Article concerns *'the abolition of existing restrictions on freedom of establishment within the Community'* (emphasis added).

The powers given in Article 54 include:

o ensuring close co-operation between member-states ((3)(b));

o abolishing administrative procedures and practices . . . which would form an obstacle to freedom of establishment (c);

o ensuring that workers can become self-employed in other member-states (d);

o 'by effecting the progressive abolition of restrictions on freedom of establishment in every branch of activity under consideration, both as regards the conditions for setting up agencies, branches or subsidiaries . . .' (f).

Only after the specific powers comes a general, subordinated power

'to co-ordinate *to the necessary extent* the safeguards which, for the protection of the interests of members and others, are required by Member-states of companies and firms . . . with a view to making such safeguards equivalent throughout the Community' ((g), emphasis added).

The Treaty power, therefore, is to co-ordinate safeguards to the necessary extent that they do not distort the Commission's general task, to promote freedom of establishment. Yet the Commission has repeatedly attempted to use it to standardise, by the 5th Company Law Directive, a particular structure of corporate management. It has never seriously argued that the difference of management structures impedes freedom of establishment in member-states.

Since the Single European Act, Article 54 measures can be achieved by *qualified majority* instead of, as formerly, requiring unanimity.

Article 100

The Commission has also used Article 100 to promote statutory 'worker participation' in companies, in the 'Vredeling' Directive. Article 100 allowed the Commission to

'issue directives for the approximation of such provisions laid down by law, regulation or administrative action in member-states as *directly affect the establishment or functioning of the common market'* (emphasis added).

Again, the Commission never seriously argued that the way in which workers are involved in the success of businesses did indeed directly affect the establishment of freedom of trade or establishment within the community. It is self-evident that there can be a miscellany of approaches—best chosen within the different businesses themselves.

It remains important to try to ensure that, although the Single European Act watered down the Treaty by allowing a qualified majority for measures

'laid down by law, regulation or administrative action in Member-states *which have as their object* the establishment or functioning of the *internal* market' (emphasis added),

unanimity is still observed as required for:

○ fiscal provisions;

○ those relating to the free movement of people;

○ those relating to the rights and interests of employed persons.

And it also remains an important point of principle that directives should be issued only to complete the internal market, not for wider purposes.

Article 118

The Commission has made much of a supposed 'social dimension' of the Economic Community. Article 118 gives the Commission limited powers in the social dimension. It is worth paying particular attention to the closely limited Treaty powers:

'Without prejudice to the other provisions of this Treaty and in conformity with its general objectives, the Commission shall have the task of promoting close co-operation in the social field, particularly in matters relating to:

○ employment;

○ labour law and working conditions;

○ basic and advanced vocational training;

○ social security;

○ prevention of occupational accidents and diseases;

○ occupational hygiene;

○ the right of association, and collective bargaining between employers and workers.'

'To this end, the Commission shall act in close contact with Member-states by making studies, delivering opinions, and arranging consultations ...' (Article 118).

Again, it is quite clear:

(a) that these powers are to be exercised in conformity with the general objects of the Treaty, i.e. promoting free trade and establishment;

(b) that the Commission's primary rôle is informational and not to standardise any particular practice by law.

The SEA, however, added Article 118(a). This says:

'Member-states shall pay particular attention to encouraging improvements, especially in the working environment, as regards the health and safety of workers, ...';

and it gives power to issue directives by qualified majority. Article 118(b) provides that:

'The Commission shall endeavour to develop the dialogue between management and labour at European level which would, if the two sides consider it desirable, lead to relations based on agreement.'

This vague language seems to be intended to promote Europe-wide collective bargaining. The Commission is, however, given no specific powers.

Conclusions

The evidence of experience with the Commission's interpretation of Articles 54, 100 and 118 suggests the following conclusions:

o the Treaty of Rome, even as amended by the SEA, gives the Commission limited legal powers and these powers all fall within the framework that they must be *necessary to complete the common market* or (for some, since the SEA) *have as their object the completion of the internal market*. It is strongly arguable that the SEA should be interpreted narrowly, within the thrust and context of the Treaty itself.

o Often the primary powers envisage other techniques than the blanket issue of directives: information, studies, promotion of co-operation. They are voluntarist. Britain should insist that these are used first, and directives as a last resort and only when proved necessary.

○ Even where directives are permitted, they should be designed to correct the particular abuses which impede freedom of trade or establishment within *particular member-states*. It is a sign of the Commission's expansionist centralism that it usually issues blanket directives to cover every member-state, rather than, for example, using powers to direct one or two states to correct legislation which is impeding the establishment of the market.

○ For some years Britain failed to have the political and legal confidence to link its vision of the Treaty to the words which the Treaty employs. They hang together, for both are liberal, free trade and free establishment. In the past, officials and ministers feared that to pick up these abuses of power would be deemed *'non communautaire'*. More recently, the Commission has become aware that each measure will be tested against the Treaty and that measures which are *ultra vires* its powers will cause real legal and political difficulty. At the same time, it has become clear that Britain is prepared to put forward alternative strategies—as in the case of the 'competing currency' approach to monetary co-operation. And it is moving to strengthen national Parliamentary supervision of Commission proposals.

All these indications suggest that it is possible to move towards a new constitutionalist approach to European co-operation, based on a strict interpretation of the Treaty powers, and a free-trade, free-establishment economic philosophy consistent with its objectives.

7

THE POWERS OF THE EUROPEAN PARLIAMENT: THE WESTMINSTER DEFICIT

Frank Vibert

Deputy Director,
Institute of Economic Affairs

Summary

THIS CHAPTER EXAMINES the case for an expansion of the powers of the European Parliament. It reviews the arguments that are put forward for such an expansion. It examines the additional functions which, it has been suggested, the European Parliament could perform, for example, in the legislative and financial areas. It also analyses the more general case for an enlarged rôle of the European Parliament which rests in part on the alleged shortcomings of Westminster (or any single legislature at the national level) in dealing with European issues. It outlines the two main ways for addressing these deficiencies, either the introduction of greater national representation into the European Parliament through the creation of a second chamber at Strasbourg, or alternatively taking steps to address 'the Westminster deficit' by making changes at Westminster itself.

The conclusions of this chapter are as follows:

o No extension of the powers of the European Parliament in legislative or budgetary areas is either warranted or desirable.

o It is also misplaced for the European Parliament to seek to enlarge its 'pre-legislative' review rôle as an attempt to share legislative responsibility with the Council of Ministers.

o Instead, the European Parliament should focus its work on its 'watch-dog' role over the European Commission in order to provide for a more systematic check against the abuse of powers by the Commission, for more rigorous scrutiny of the effectiveness (or lack thereof) of Community spending programmes, and to form an extra line of defence against market interventionism and the imposition of external trade barriers.

o At the same time, there is an urgency to strengthening Westminster's capacity to deal with European issues.

o Redressing this 'Westminster deficit' involves a willingness to see institutional changes in the way European issues are handled in both the House of Commons and the House of Lords.*

o Protecting and enhancing the rôle of national parliaments will also involve revisions in Europe's treaties in order to introduce the concept of 'legislative reserve' so as to better defend the interests of member-states and their electorates and to provide a check against the centralising tendencies of Community institutions.

o Finally, with these changes, there is no rôle or place for a second European chamber in Strasbourg.

This chapter makes specific suggestions on how the 'watch-dog' rôle of the European Parliament can be made more effective as well as how to redress the Westminster deficit. Such changes should be seen as part of the necessity to base co-operation in Europe on a solid constitutional foundation built on vigorous democratic practices within member-states. Freedom in Europe is best guaranteed by a diffusion of power. The parliamentary frameworks of member-states need to be kept firm against erosion by the latent legislative activism and unbounded spending ambitions of a more powerful European Parliament.

I. THE REASONS FOR ENLARGING THE ROLE OF THE EUROPEAN PARLIAMENT

Several member-states of the European Community are suggesting an enlargement of the powers of the European Parliament. There are three distinct strands in the arguments advanced in favour of increased powers:

*See note 10, below, page 113.

o First, there are some who see a larger rôle for the European Parliament as part of the architecture of European 'union'. According to this view, progress in implementing the Single Market should be matched by steps to strengthen the Community's political institutions.

o Secondly, there are expressions of concern about a 'democratic deficit'. Proponents of this view foresee the desirability of more decisions on Europe's future being taken at the Community level as well as increasing powers being wielded by the unelected bureaucracy of the European Commission. The inference is drawn that these trends create a 'democratic deficit' which ought to be redressed by a more powerful European Parliament. From its own perspective, the Commission itself points to a 'democratic deficit'. It naturally wishes to see an increase in its own powers and it views a more powerful European Parliament as an ally in restraining the Council of Ministers, thus leading to a further enhancement of its own rôle in providing political direction in the Community.

o Thirdly, geopolitical concerns centring around events in Eastern Europe and Germany have prompted some observers to advocate a strengthening of Community institutions, including the Parliament. In the view of these observers, such a development would help provide a 'solid core' for Europe at a time of instability. It would bolster the 'magnet effect' of the Community in drawing the countries of Eastern Europe towards the West, help 'anchor' Germany[1] as well as provide a counterweight to what is foreseen to be a weaker NATO alliance.

Such arguments can mislead. Nor do the inferences necessarily follow from the diagnosis. Progress in implementing and enlarging the Single Market and in reducing external barriers to trade are not necessarily, to say the least, going to be supported by movement towards centralising structures in Europe. On the contrary, it can be argued with equal or greater force that centralising tendencies are likely to work against market-oriented structures. Central bodies are inherently prone to intervene and to destroy the vitality that comes

---

[1] 'Anchoring' Germany is a euphemism for two different concerns: one, that Germany could float off into a neutralist middle Europe; the second, that Germany could come to dominate Western Europe and thus needs to be folded within more broadly based political institutions such as provided by a more powerful European Parliament.

from competing political jurisdictions. Open markets in Europe which should result from the implementation of the Single Market programme will check government intervention and bureaucratic regulation at the national level. Those who wish to restore the possibilities for intervention and regulatory interference are precisely those who advocate stronger central community structures.

Redefining the EC's Rôle to Remove the 'Democratic Deficit'

Not only are centralising inferences unwarranted but so, too, are the inferences of those who diagnose a 'democratic deficit'. It was argued in Chapter 4 that, when looked at as constitutional documents, Community Treaties are profoundly defective. Redressing the constitutional deficit involves eliminating the political rôle ascribed to the Commission in the Treaties as well as other Treaty revisions. These would provide an alternative framework for institutional development in Europe not necessarily leading to the conclusion that the powers of the European Parliament need to be enlarged. The so-called 'democratic deficit' can be addressed by a redefinition of the rôle of the Commission, which would emphasise its function as a civil service and agency for the member-states of the Council and remove its aspirations to provide central political direction.

Geopolitical concerns also do not lead to any inevitable conclusion that the powers of the European Parliament should be enlarged. The political priority for countries in Eastern Europe is the re-establishment of democratic practices and frameworks within their own boundaries. Germany has its own internal dynamic and an external dimension relating to the security arrangements in Europe properly addressed in other contexts such as NATO. The diffusion of power in Europe, through maintaining the vitality of the democratic institutions of member-states and through constitutional limits on community bodies, provides a more potent way of assuaging concerns about whether one country (or small group of countries) can come to dominate Western Europe than through enlarging the powers of the European Parliament. The rôle of the European Parliament, therefore, should be considered on its own merits and without the foregone conclusions of those supporting increased European centralisation, whether wrapped in 'union' clothing or cloaked in the 'democratic deficit'.

The analysis of this paper also avoids the terminology of 'sovereignty' and related expressions such as the 'transfer of sovereignty' or the 'pooling of sovereignty'. Such phrases can be used by both proponents of greater power for the European Parliament as well as by opponents as much as to conceal the underlying issues as to illuminate them.[2] The crucial distinction is between those proposals for European institutions which would centralise power in the Community in contrast to those proposals which would diffuse it.

Thus, the approach taken in this paper is, first, to examine those specific areas of responsibility where it has been suggested that the European Parliament could extend its rôle and, second, the more general argument that is made on the grounds that national frameworks can no longer deal effectively with European issues—a diagnosis referred to as 'the Westminster deficit'.

II. THE POWERS OF THE EUROPEAN PARLIAMENT—POSSIBLE AREAS FOR EXTENSION

There are three main areas where it has been suggested that the powers of the European Parliament could be extended. These are:

o to have a more active legislative rôle;

o to have enlarged responsibilities for the Community budget;

o to broaden its powers of scrutiny and review.

Each of these potential areas and the rationale for an extension of powers is discussed below in relation to the present functions of the European Parliament.

(i) The Legislative Rôle

Currently the European Parliament's legislative rôle is restricted. Under the single reading procedure, it has the right to propose amendments to legislation under consideration by the Council,[3] but the Council is free to accept or reject them as it feels fit. The rôle of the European Parliament is thus consultative. Under the two reading co-operation procedure relevant to Single Market legislation, the rôle of

---

[2] The terms 'federal' and 'confederal' are also avoided because of their ambiguity. For example, 'federal' means a system of centralised powers to some and shared powers to others.

[3] Which will eventually appear in the form of regulations which enter into effect when published in the *Official Journal* of the Community or directives which require appropriate implementing action by member-states.

the European Parliament goes beyond consultation on the first reading to the possibility of introducing (re-introducing) amendments at the second reading stage to a 'common position' adopted by the Council. If the European Parliament's amendment is accepted by the Commission, it takes unanimity on the part of the Council to override the amendment and in the event there is not unanimity in the Council, the European Parliament has thus the potential to make an impact on legislation.

Three main reasons are advanced why the legislative rôle of the European Parliament should be extended beyond this presently limited power of amendment and confer on the European Parliament the right to initiate and to enact legislation. First, there are 'practical' considerations. It is claimed that reliance on individual member-states (rather than on a common European legislature) to enact Council directives leads to considerable delays in implementation (as is currently the case for some member-states in the implementation of Single Market directives). Moreover, it is said that relying on action by member-states incurs the risk of variations in what is implemented which may defeat the common objectives. Both these risks are seen as likely to increase if the Community is further enlarged to include new member-states in one form of association or another.

A second view looks to US practices and envisages that the European Parliament should, in the fullness of time, aspire to the rôle of the US Congress and perform a legislative function, while the Council would perform an executive rôle similar in concept to the US Presidency.

A third view is that by virtue of direct election, the European Parliament has a legitimacy in representing a 'European' perspective which counteracts the member-state perspectives of Council members and which should be reflected in a shared legislative responsibility on European matters.

The first of these views, the perceived 'impracticality' of current arrangements, does not appear compelling. The Council has power of persuasion with member-states that fall behind in implementing directives, market forces will tend to encourage harmonisation and convergence and, as a last resort, there is legal sanction through national courts or the Court of Justice. Enlargement will not invalidate this general approach.

As far as the two other views outlined above are concerned, any shift of legislative functions to the European Parliament would entail resolving certain fundamental issues:

o First, there is the problem of demarcation between the sphere of legislative responsibility of the European Parliament and the sphere of responsibility of national parliaments in a way which will not lead to a gradual (or rapid) withering of the vigour of parliamentary institutions within member-states because of legislative activism from the centre. Jacques Delors points to the principle of 'subsidiarity' as providing an answer. No definition of subsidiarity, however, has yet been put forward which in itself provides the safeguards necessary and which could be enforced in constitutional law.[4] At a time when the institutions of representative government are being re-established in the countries of Eastern Europe, it would provide the worst possible example to risk eroding them in the countries of Western Europe.

o Secondly, any shared responsibility for legislation between the Council of Ministers and the European Parliament inevitably entails a fairly complicated procedure for resolving differences between the two bodies (through conference, veto and override procedures). Even if these can be established, the end-result is a blurring of responsibility for legislation with a consequential loss of accountability to voters.[5] A combination of centralisation in the Community together with a blurring of accountability hardly seems a prescription for democratic advancement in Europe.

o Thirdly, a legislative rôle for the European Parliament implies a very fundamental departure from the kind of rôle played by national legislatures in Europe *vis-à-vis* their executives. National assemblies in Europe provide governments with majorities by which legislation can be passed after debate and scrutiny. Governments resign if they cannot command a majority. The rôle of the US Congress and its relationship with the executive is quite different. While there may be good reason to depart from the kinds of parliamentary systems existing in Western Europe in order to move towards a US congressional system, it is incumbent on those who would support this evolution to prove their point rather than simply to assert it on the grounds that it is good for European 'union'. The claim of the European Parliament for a legislative rôle

---

[4] See 'Note on "Subsidiarity"' (Annex 1, below, page 118).

[5] It also opens the door wide to interest-group politics, already becoming a factor in Brussels and Strasbourg. A code of conduct for MEPs is probably timely.

rests on no firmer a basis than the belief that it has a legitimacy to act on European issues which transcends that of national parliaments and the views of member-states as reflected in the Council. There is no reason to accept this claim. Europe is what its constituent member-states wish to make of it. If the vision of the member-states is to maintain a Europe of cultural diversity and a democratic diffusion of power, there is every reason not to aggrandise the European Parliament.

(ii) Power of the Purse

A second area where it has been suggested that an extension of the powers of the European Parliament would be appropriate is in connection with the Community budget. Currently, the powers of the European Parliament are limited in several respects. Revenues must be decided by the Council and derived from national budgets and taxation systems and thus must be approved by national parliaments under national procedures. In addition, about three-quarters of Community expenditures currently fall into a category of so-called 'compulsory expenditures' on which the European Parliament can propose modifications but which can be subsequently rejected by the Council. Where the European Parliament gains some leverage is in respect of so-called 'non-compulsory expenditures' where it can propose amendments to the Council (subject in theory to a specified maximum increase over the previous year but in practice the limit may be modified). It also gains leverage because the Parliament must adopt the budget as a whole or reject it. (However, in cases where the budget has not been adopted, the Council is able to continue to authorise expenditures under Article 204.)

Budget procedures have in practice led to an almost predictable annual confrontation between Council and Parliament. While these have momentarily abated as a result of an understanding between Council, Commission and Parliament, nevertheless, the history shows that the motivation behind the European Parliament's critiques of Community budgets has not been a concern to limit the growth of the Community's budget. Instead, the conflicts have arisen because of the Parliament's attempts to increase overall expenditure, its own budgetary powers and in particular the 'non-compulsory expenditures' where it can propose amendments.

The rationale for an extension of the budget powers of the European Parliament is the perception that Community expenditure programmes will be growing rapidly in future years (for example, as proposed by the Commission for regional programmes and for Eastern Europe). It is argued that since parliamentary control over such expenditures cannot be exercised by any individual national parliament, it properly falls to the European Parliament to exercise this function. Thus it is suggested that the European Parliament should have the specific possibilities to determine the overall size of the budget and all categories of expenditure within the total. On the revenue side, it would determine the size of contributions under the Community's 'own resources', the source of those contributions (for example, whether VAT or GNP related) as well as gain the power to raise new taxes and to tax and collect directly.

At first sight, the case for giving the European Parliament a measure of greater financial responsibility for the Community budget would appear plausible. But a more considered view would reveal some basic difficulties. First, there is the problem that the European Parliament is likely to reflect a strong upward spending bias in encouraging expanded Community programmes. Not only is there an institutional bias in this direction but several of the Community spending programmes (both regional funds and agricultural subsidies are examples) have all the classic ingredients of 'pork barrel' programmes with appeal to special interests that make a mockery of spending constraint.

In theory the restraining factor on the spending ambitions of elected assemblies is provided by the need to raise taxes which in turn have to be justified to the reluctant electorate. The logic of this constraint argues that if the European Parliament is to have increased powers over spending, it must have a corresponding responsibility for taxation. There are two objections to conceding a power to tax to the European Parliament. First, the need for governments to raise money has been the historical foundation for the power of national parliaments and a transfer of taxation responsibilities strikes at a very basic element underpinning the rôle of national parliaments. Secondly, the conferring of tax powers on the European Parliament will act as a constraint on spending ambitions only if the electorate is able to draw a clear and transparent connection between the spending side of the European Parliament's budget functions and the taxation side. However, this transparent connection is likely to be missing. Instead, there is likely to be a continuous struggle between the European Parliament and the Council with each side able to cast 'blame' on the other for the eventual taxation consequences. Neither present budget procedures in the European Parliament nor US experience of budgetary struggles between Congress and the Presidency offers encouragement that transparent procedures for pin-pointing responsibility can be found.

Both of these concerns might be met if the constraint on the latent spending propensity of the European Parliament were set not in terms of a corresponding taxation responsibility but through constitutional limits perhaps embodied in future Treaty revisions.[6] While Treaty revision probably should contain constitutional constraints on Community spending, unfortunately not too much reliance can be placed on them. Whatever limit is set is likely to be fully exploited by the spending bias of the European Parliament and subject to constant upward pressure. What is intended to be a ceiling will always be treated as a floor. US experience with Gramm/Rudman/Hollings points to the difficulty not only of expressing budget constraint in ways that are valid from a constitutional point of view, but also the difficulty of controlling 'loopholes'. 'Off budget' techniques, the exploitation of borrowing or guarantee programmes (which defer obligations), and the inherent margins of error in estimation techniques on both the revenue and spending sides, are just three of the loopholes that make non-tax budget limits so difficult to apply when faced with spending pressure.

A European Parliament with increased powers over the Community budget will inevitably mean ever-increasing spending at the Community level, a high-tax Europe and a loss of accountability to the taxpayer.

(iii) Scrutiny and Review

In assessing the rôle of the European Parliament in scrutiny and review of Community affairs, it is useful to distinguish between review prior to legislation being finalised by the Council ('pre-legislative' review), scrutiny at the time of enactment of regulations, and later review of the effects of Community decisions (downstream or *ex-post* review).

The focus of activity by the European Parliament is currently on the 'pre-legislative' review rôle. This is undertaken through a range of subject-oriented Committees (18 in all) that review Commission proposals to the Council (including the legal basis) and question and

---

[6] This would involve elaborating Article 199 which calls for expenditure and revenue to be in balance. This Article has not itself proved effective because, *inter alia*, spending pressures have been continually accommodated by revenue increases.

collect evidence, primarily from Commissioners and Commission staff, but also from outside witnesses.

As far as downstream or *ex-post* review is concerned, the focus is set primarily in narrow accounting terms centred on the budget discharge procedure (Article 206(b)) which incorporates the report of the Court of Auditors. Review in this accounting sense is the subject of one of the 18 specialised review committees—the Budgetary Control Committee. Although the reports of the Court of Auditors can range more broadly, they are cast primarily in a traditional audit framework checking that revenue and expenditures are received and incurred 'in a lawful and regular manner' (Article 206(a)2).

In looking at whether the European Parliament's activities in the area of scrutiny and review should be extended, the Parliament has placed emphasis on strengthening its 'pre-legislative' rôle. In particular, MEPs object to the 'closed door' negotiations that take place between member-governments (at Civil Service working party stages, COREPER consideration and at the full Council) in drawing up Council proposals and in considering European Parliament amendments to proposed Council decisions.

Underlying the desire of MEPs and the European Parliament to see its mandate extended in this direction is the desire to bolster the legislative and financial powers of the Parliament and to share them with the Council. As discussed earlier, neither development would be desirable.

The ambition of the European Parliament to assure itself of at least a shared responsibility for legislation with the Council, finds an ally in the Commission which would also like to maintain its aspirations to provide political direction in the Community. This alliance between Parliament and the Commission may also feature in the 'co-operation' procedure on Single Market legislation where the Commission has gained an undesirable 'middleman' rôle in accepting or objecting to amendments made by the Parliament to Council proposals.

Related to this desire of the European Parliament to increase its pre-legislative rôle, if necessary in alliance with the Commission, is its desire to have the power to approve senior Community appointments—particularly the appointments of Commissioners and the Head of Commission. Under current arrangements, the European Parliament has no formal rôle in this process.[7] But it does possess the

---

[7] As a way of asserting its aspirations, the Parliament does in fact vote to 'approve' an incoming Commission.

power through a special majority to censure the Commission (in which case it must resign *en bloc*).[8] This power has never been used and for a variety of reasons is somewhat of an empty threat.

Implicit in this desire of the European Parliament to approve appointments to the Commission and to approve the programme of an incoming Commission is in part the view that the Commission should also provide political direction for the Community. While this rôle was indeed envisaged in the Treaties, it has been argued elsewhere[9] that such a rôle for the Commission is completely inappropriate and should be remedied as part of the Treaty revision process. If the Commission evolves as a body providing a civil service and agency function for the Council of Ministers, then there will not be a programme to approve independent of the agenda items under consideration by the Council. Moreover, since Commissioners and other senior Community appointments should be appointed on the basis of administrative merit including private sector experience, the more such appointments are depoliticised the better. This would argue against any involvement in such appointments by the European Parliament.

Because of the Parliament's pursuit of its pre-legislative rôle and its desire to share powers with the Council—if necessary, in alliance with the Commission—the result has been the neglect of two other dimensions of scrutiny and review. The first is the potential rôle that the European Parliament could play in limiting the tendency of the Commission to step beyond its powers both in the initiation and proposal process and in regulatory matters. Secondly, there is a need to broaden the downstream review process to move beyond accounting and audit concepts of review to scrutiny in the sense of evaluating the economic effectiveness of Community programmes, particularly spending programmes. The cost to the consumers of the CAP, the rates of return earned on regional fund expenditures—these are the types of question that need more attention and where the European Parliament could use its existing powers more usefully. Its existing committees could spend more time on downstream scrutiny. In addition, the Parliament has the right to demand reports from the Commission providing for *ex-post* evaluations of Community programmes.

---

[8] A motion of censure must be carried by a two-thirds majority of the votes cast, representing a majority of the Members of the European Parliament.

[9] See Chapter 6, above, pp. 74 *et seq.*

Limitations to the European Parliament's Checking Rôle

In considering the effectiveness of the European Parliament in providing a checking mechanism on the Commission, there are, however, two areas where its rôle may be hampered by the existing language of the Treaties. One instance is in respect of Articles 237 and 238 which give the Parliament the right to ratify Agreements and Treaties between the Community and other countries and organisations. Important in this context is the rôle of these Articles in respect of external trade agreements between the Community and third parties. There are a number of protectionist measures which the Commission may wish to adopt which could fall short of formal agreements of the sort coming within the scope of these Articles—for example, voluntary export restraints adopted by a third party under pressure from the Commission. Neither is it clear that other forms of protection, such as the imposition of anti-dumping or European content regulations, are properly cross-referenced between Articles 113, 115, and 238. Here the Parliament's review rôle is not only important in respect of the need for the Community to maintain open external trading arrangements but also because the market distortions introduced by trade barriers have an uneven impact within the Community and are a source of friction between member-states.

A second area where the scrutiny and review rôles of the European Parliament may be impeded by the language of the Treaties is in respect of Articles 173 and 175 which relate to the parties bringing suit and the grounds on which suit may be brought before the Court of Justice for reviewing the legality of acts of the Council and Commission. The current language of Article 175 enables the Parliament to bring action against the Commission for 'failure to act'. However, in order to provide the Parliament with more effective means of checking the Commission, Article 173 needs to be amended to enable the Parliament to bring action against the Commission for exceeding its powers (*ultra vires*).

$$*\qquad*\qquad*\qquad*\qquad*$$

This review of the specific areas of possible extension of the powers of the European Parliament suggests that the arguments in favour of new powers are ill-founded. However, the more general case can still be made that enlarged powers for the European Parliament are required because of the inability of national assemblies singly to deal effectively with collective European issues. This is considered next in the context of Westminster.

III. THE WESTMINSTER DEFICIT

The arguments that have been reviewed about the powers of the European Parliament have concerned specific functions and areas of responsibility. There is, however, a different type of argument. This one relates to the alleged deficiencies of Westminster. It is argued that Westminster is ineffective in dealing with Community matters and inherently unable to provide effective scrutiny and control of European issues.

There are several elements in this case. It is said that Westminster's system for the review and scrutiny of European legislation does not provide for effective 'pre-legislative' review at the formative stage. Moreover, the European Parliament is inherently better placed to carry out such review by virtue of its proximity to and close relationship with the Commission, COREPER and Council committees. The links which Westminster has to Europe are said to be weak, particularly with the decline of dual mandate MPs, and Westminster is thus said to be 'out of touch' with trends in thinking in other European countries, with no very obvious way of remedy. Furthermore, the kind of Ministerial accountability which Westminster provides through floor debates and the debative questioning of Ministers is said to have lost much of its relevance in respect of European issues as a result of the greater use of majority voting in the Council of Ministers where Britain's own ministers can be outvoted. As European issues gather in importance and begin to permeate every area of life from domestic issues to foreign policy issues, and the more they are addressed through the Community, the greater become the deficiencies at Westminster.

There are two very different responses to these perceptions. One response (with a post-war history that goes back to the 1950s European Defence Community) is to accept the logic for strengthening the European Parliament but to argue that its increased functions should be exercised through a bicameral system (a second chamber in Strasbourg). The other response is to try to cure Westminster's deficiencies (in so far as they exist) at Westminster itself. Each of these two approaches is outlined below.

(i) A Second Chamber at Strasbourg?

Two distinct versions of a second chamber at Strasbourg have been proposed at times in the past. They correspond to two different views of the rôle of a second chamber. One view is that the second chamber needs to provide a means to strengthen the voice of member-states through their elected parliamentary representatives. Thus members of national parliaments might be sent (probably by indirect election according to party strength in national assemblies) to form a second chamber. The purpose of this would be to improve the popular representative quality of the European Parliament. The other view is that the second house should reflect the voice of member-states as represented by their governments. Thus, the second chamber would be made up of ministerial-level appointees with special responsibilities for Europe. This prescription accepts that governments as represented in the Council are too preoccupied with a national perspective. A permanent ministerial presence in Strasbourg would enable a 'more European' view of matters to be taken as well as ultimately a better understanding of the different positions of the governments of member-states.

Common to both approaches, however, is an underlying assumption that, as presently constituted, the European Parliament does not have a valid claim to represent Europe. On the one hand, it is an elected body. On the other, it does not reflect adequately the weight of views in member-states. The underlying issue is that the representatives chosen by electorates for their national parliaments may reflect a composition quite different from the pattern of collective representation at Strasbourg. The governments commanding majorities in national parliaments may also face quite different and possibly hostile majorities in Strasbourg. While constitutional government can allow for power to be shared between authorities elected by different electorates, the present relationship between the European Parliament and national assemblies and governments is not satisfactory. It is felt, probably correctly, that unless the 'mismatching' of representation is in some way modified, in order to achieve a closer correspondence with the views of member-states, there will always be a tenuous connection between member-states and the European Parliament, a problem in the acceptability of according greater powers to Strasbourg and an inherent institutional fragility.

The case, however, for attempting to redress these problems by constructing a second chamber for the European Parliament rests on two assumptions. First, that there are additional powers that should be wielded by the European Parliament. A review of the specific functions in question has shown that this assumption is false. The second assumption is that the deficiencies in national parliaments which prevent them from coming to grips effectively with European issues cannot be addressed by changes, where necessary, in the way national parliaments conduct their European business. As far as Westminster is concerned, this second assumption is also false. There are ways of curing the 'Westminster deficit'. These are examined below.

(ii) Curing the Westminster Deficit

There are three areas where Westminster's capacity to play an effective rôle in European matters can be improved:

o In the 'pre-legislative' area where policy can be discussed at a formative stage;

o In the 'representational' area where Westminster needs to be better informed of views in other member-states;

o In the area of protecting the prerogatives of member-states where the concept of 'legislative reserve' needs to be introduced into Community treaties along with other 'reserve' mechanisms.

The pre-legislative area has been the focus particularly of a recent report of the House of Commons Select Committee on Procedure. It has made a number of recommendations designed to enable the House of Commons better to follow issues while they are still at a formative stage. Probably the most important of these is the recommendation that there should be Special Standing Committees established to question Ministers on forthcoming policy issues. The kind of questioning envisaged is of an 'investigative' nature rather than the 'debative' questioning familiar in Question Time on the floor of the House.

The recommendation in favour of Special Standing Committees will not be an easy one for the government (or any government) to accept. There is an inherent discomfort in any government agreeing to its Ministers being subject to additional scrutiny. There is a traditional concern to have scrutiny exercised through debates on the floor of the House rather than through Committee questioning; the switch of emphasis from debative questioning to investigative questioning is in some respects more difficult for a government to handle; and, finally, there will be a fear that Ministers will find themselves boxed into a position ahead of the give-and-take at a Council meeting in Brussels. However, the overriding consideration must be the need to show that the House of Commons can investigate European issues in depth at a formative stage. Failure in this respect makes the case for the European Parliament to extend its pre-legislative rôle that much stronger. Therefore, this recommendation of the Select Committee on Procedure should be accepted along with the other recommendations.[10]

As far as improving the representational quality of Westminster is concerned, the need is to make sure that Westminster is fully aware of and perhaps better attuned to opinion in other member-states of the Community (regardless of whether Parliament happens to agree with it or not). The government is generally aware of the attitude of other member-states through regular Council meetings and other Community forums. The same is probably not the case for Westminster as a whole. The obvious channel for improving communication is through MEPs. There are good reasons why MEPs should not be accorded any formal status in the House of Commons. Membership in the House of Commons is conferred by the electorate and even part-membership is not to be conferred by the House—to mention but one. The same electoral considerations do not apply, however, to the House of Lords. The representative quality of the House of Lords would be improved (and could not possibly suffer) if non-attending hereditary peers were disbarred from attendance and MEPs were allowed rights as members (without titles) for debates on European issues or as part-members by being allowed to participate fully in the proceedings of the Select Committee on the European Communities. This would introduce the perspective they can bring to Westminster of the views of other member-states as reflected in Strasbourg, as well as their future experience in holding the Commission to account. It would not upset the constitutional balance between the two Houses which bedevils most House of Lords reform proposals.

'Legislative Reserve' and Opting Out

The final issue is that no matter how well Westminster covers European issues, its efforts will inevitably be wasted because

---

[10] Select Committee on Procedure, *The Working of the Select Committee*, Session 1989-90, HC 19, London: HMSO, 1990. The Government has subsequently announced its acceptance of the main recommendations in this report. (This chapter is a revised version of the paper first published as *IEA Inquiry* No. 16 in March 1990.)

Community matters are increasingly decided by majority voting in which British ministers can be outvoted. In this context it was mentioned in Chapter 6 (pp. 80-83) that among the defects of Europe's treaties are inadequate safeguards for member-states that are outvoted. Among the Treaty revisions that can address this problem is provision for 'legislative reserve'. Under such a procedure, a member-state that is outvoted in the Council may give its assent to the measure subject to approval by its legislature and otherwise opt out.[11] The possibility of 'opting out' is crucial not only for protecting the rights of member-states; it also provides a check on majorities from attempting to override minorities on the Council. Where the majority goes in one direction and a minority of member-states goes in another, the different approaches are subject to valid testing in the different political jurisdictions.

Changes in each of the three areas discussed above would improve the ability of Westminster to make an effective and informed contribution on European matters. They are changes that may not be entirely comfortable for Westminster. The alternative, however, is a strengthening of the voice of those who argue that Westminster is ineffective and out of touch. The alternative remedy proposed by such voices is much less palatable—the creation of a second house for the European Parliament. It involves the much worse prospect of permanent damage to British institutions through a gradual ceding of powers to Strasbourg.

Arguments put forward in favour of maintaining and enhancing the ability of national frameworks to deal with European issues are sometimes dismissed as failing to recognise European interdependence. This is misrepresentation. The debate about European structures is about the diffusion of powers as compared with centralisation. National parliamentary frameworks provide by far the most effective basis for diffused powers in Europe.

IV. CONCLUSIONS AND RECOMMENDATIONS

Conclusions

The agenda for co-operation in Europe in the 1990s is a full one. In order to fulfil the objectives of the Single Market programme in the Community, action extending beyond 1992 will be required; the area

---

[11] See 'Note on Constitutional "Reserves"' (Annex 2, below, page 119).

of the Single Market itself needs to be broadened and different types of association and membership arrangements forged between the Community with EFTA and countries in Eastern Europe. Changes in the structure of NATO will be required and new rôles may need to be played by the Council of Europe and the Western European Union.

At first sight, the idea that these changes could be facilitated by a stronger European Parliament with greater legislative and financial powers appears attractive. On closer inspection it is the reverse of what is required. The mistake would be compounded by establishing a second chamber for the European Parliament. Legislative powers for the European Parliament will be difficult to contain within any defined bounds. Their exercise will lead to a rapid erosion of the rôle of national parliaments. Additional financial authority for the European Parliament will unleash spending propensities without effective means of limitation. This too will lead to a further undermining of the rôle of national parliamentary institutions. The result will be to make government remote from the people, to blur responsibilities, and to diminish accountability. Democratic institutions that have been built up in member-states over generations will be weakened, and in cases where such institutions are new or are being re-established, their development will be discouraged. The best protection for individual liberties and for the vitality of Europe's diversity is through a diffusion of political power and not through centralisation.

In order to deal flexibly with Europe's agenda for the 1990s, it is the democratic frameworks of Europe's member-states that need to be strengthened and in particular their capacity to handle European issues. Maintaining the vigour of national parliaments will involve introducing the concept of legislative 'reserve' into the Community Treaties as well as additional forms of 'reserve'. But other measures need not await Treaty revision. To correct the Westminster deficit further, the recommendations of the House of Commons Select Committee on Procedure should be implemented* and in particular the Government should accept the setting up of Special Standing Committees on European legislative areas. The introduction of MEPs into full or part membership of Westminster's second chamber (the House of Lords) is a further step which would strengthen the European dimension of Westminster's work. Such a step would improve the representative quality of the House of Lords without affecting the constitutional balance between the two Houses.

---

*See note 10, above, page 113.

The European Parliament can play its part by defining its rôle in ways supportive of national parliamentary frameworks. It should rid itself of the conceit that it represents a more valid view of Europe's future than the views expressed by member-states through their Council and through their parliaments. This means the European Parliament must move away from seeking to prize out a legislative and financial rôle from member-states. It should distance itself from the concept that it is an ally of the Commission in attempting to wrest powers from the European Council. Instead it should exercise a watch-dog rôle over the Commission. It should act to give first warning to member-states if Community spending programmes are ineffective or going astray and have authority at law to restrain the Commission from acting beyond its powers. It should see its *raison d'être* to use its review and scrutiny function to guard against Commission interference in the Single Market and in open external trading arrangements. Within this setting, its rôle must be to support the effective functioning of the competing political jurisdictions of member-states rather than to try to build a new centralism. A European superstate is a false god. Efforts to build up centralising institutions take Europe down the wrong path.

Recommendations

To address the Westminster deficit:

1. Adopt recommendations of Select Committee on Procedure for House of Commons.

2. Introduce MEPs into House of Lords as full or as Select Committee members.

3. Incorporate mechanism of legislative reserve (and other reserves) into Community Treaties.

To refocus the work of the European Parliament:

1. Substitute 'failure to act' by 'acts beyond powers' as grounds for parliament to bring Commission before Court of Justice.

2. Revise treaty articles relating to review of trade barriers.

3. Institute procedures for review of programme effectiveness.

The changes identified here for parliamentary frameworks are not the only changes required for effective co-operation in Europe. Neither are the Treaty changes discussed here the only revisions needed to

Community Treaties.[12] But the changes identified to correct the Westminster deficit and to refocus the work of the European Parliament together will make future co-operation in Europe more effective, more closely linked to the peoples of Europe, and a firm bastion for a defence of their liberties.

---

[12] The next paper, published here as Chapter 8, brings together the themes of this Chapter and that of Chapter 6 within the broader context of constitutional re-arrangements for the Community.

117

ANNEX 1

Note on 'Subsidiarity'

1. Four different definitions of 'subsidiarity' are given below:

(i) The European Parliament

'The union shall only act to carry out those tasks which may be undertaken more effectively in common than by the member-states acting separately, in particular those whose execution requires action by the union because their dimensions or effects extend beyond national frontiers.'

Draft treaty establishing the European Union adopted by the European Parliament on 14 February 1984 (Article 12).

(ii) The Commission

'This is the principle which states that decisions should be taken as near as possible to the point of application. Decisions which can be taken at a local level should be taken there and not at a regional level.'

Jacques Delors, London, 1 December 1989.

(iii) British MEP

'It means that the central power shall only act in matters more effectively carried out in common than by the constituent states separately.'

Christopher Jackson, MEP, 1 February 1990 (letter to the Financial Times*).*

(iv) An IEA View

'Never allow a higher-level institutional body to undertake a task that a lower-level body could accomplish just as well.'

Victoria Curzon-Price in Whose Europe—Competing Visions for 1992, *IEA Readings No. 29, IEA, August 1989, p. 24.*

2. The principle of 'subsidiarity' is often advanced as a way of providing for an effective demarcation of the spheres within which Community institutions should work while preserving the rôle of national institutions. This claim should be treated with extreme caution. First, definitions differ, as can be seen by the four

examples cited above. Secondly, some of the definitions clearly give an open-ended licence (as with the formulations above of the European Parliament and the British MEP) which can be interpreted in ways to justify any activity being undertaken at the Community level. Thirdly, even what appear at first sight as somewhat more restrictive definitions are capable of ambiguous interpretation (for example, phrases such as 'as near as possible'). Moreover, none of the definitions cited offers a firm legal basis for demarcating responsibilities. Incorporation into the Treaties for the purpose of enforcement at law is a *sine qua non* if such a principle is to play a rôle in defining institutional responsibilities.

There may be formulations which can yet be devised which would overcome the difficulties indicated above. Even in such a case, the principle cannot be relied upon alone as a means of limiting the aspirations of community institutions. It would have to be supported by other Treaty revisions such as the elimination of the political rôle of the Commission, a strengthening of *'ultra vires'* provisions in the Treaties as well as the incorporation into the Treaties of the concept of legislative, executive and popular reserves and other derogation and opting-out procedures. Finally, the vigour of parliamentary institutions within member-states should not be put at risk in the first place.

ANNEX 2

Note on Constitutional 'Reserves'

Chapter 6, 'Europe's Constitutional Deficit', noted that existing Community Treaties do not allow for opting out and derogation. In addition, the veto procedure enshrined in the Luxembourg compromise is an unwritten and uncertain one. Constitutional reserves provide one mechanism for 'opting out' and derogation procedures. If linked to unanimity requirements, they may lead to a veto over action by other states. In other formulations they allow the dissenting government to opt out, and for other governments to go ahead if they wish. Three types of reserve can be distinguished:

○ **Executive Reserve**
The government has a veto power. The Luxembourg compromise

is one form of such an executive reserve (the US Presidential veto is another form of qualified reserve). The disadvantage of the executive reserve is that it may appear an arbitrary use of executive power. In cases where it is tied to a procedure for unanimity, it may block the path of others who wish to proceed in their own jurisdictions.

○ **Legislative Reserve**
In this case a government makes its own approval subject to approval by its parliament which, if not given, leads the agreement to fall away or prevents its application in the jurisdiction concerned. US executive branch procedures for agreeing to international financial arrangements 'subject to appropriation by Congress' is one example of legislative reserve. In the case of European Community member-states, it would be up to the government concerned as to whether to use its parliamentary majority to secure assent. A negative parliamentary vote would strengthen the hand of the dissenting government in the Council.

○ **Popular Reserve**
In this case government approval is subject to popular referendum. The best-known example is Article 89 of the Swiss Confederation:

'Federal laws and decrees of general import shall be submitted for adoption or rejection by the people when such a demand is made by 30,000 active citizens.'

Given Britain's own parliamentary traditions, the legislative reserve may appear more appropriate than the popular reserve for introduction into revised Community Treaties. However, probably each form of reserve should have its place.

8

THE NEW EUROPE: CONSTITUTIONALIST OR CENTRALIST?

Frank Vibert

Deputy Director,
Institute of Economic Affairs

Summary

THIS CHAPTER EXAMINES two alternative patterns of institutional development for the European Community. One model (referred to as the 'centralist' model) involves building up the central institutions of the Community in a power-sharing arrangement between Council, Commission and European Parliament. The other model (referred to as the 'constitutionalist' model) is one of diffused powers. In this model the European Council and Council of Ministers are the key bodies for collective decision-taking by the Community while the democratic systems in member-states provide the basis for diffused powers. This model would preserve different jurisdictions for the expression of different political preferences in Europe and for the testing of different policies. It would encourage democratic diversity in Europe.

After outlining the salient features of each model, the paper discusses the different theoretical considerations underlying the two and then outlines certain practical considerations, for example, dismissing the claim that the constitutionalist model would reduce the momentum for co-operation in Europe.

The theme of the chapter is that there exists today a possibly unique opportunity to reshape Europe and its institutions. As a result of the breakdown of post-war barriers in Europe, the Community itself needs to be reshaped as part of the revised architecture for the new Europe. The constitutional provisions of the existing Treaties are flawed. They do not provide a suitable basis for the co-operation now possible in a wider European setting and which will need to cover a broader range of issues, including, eventually, aspects of defence and security arrangements in Europe.

The chapter recommends the constitutionalist model as providing a more robust framework for taking advantage of Europe's new opportunities. The centralist model, which involves a distinction between 'senior' level central institutions of the Community and 'junior' level status for the institutions of member-states (their parliaments), is the wrong course to follow. Discussions on institutional changes in the Community will begin later this year. This chapter recommends that Heads of Governments insist that such discussions should consider constitutional issues in as wide a framework as possible.

I. INTRODUCTION

Two earlier chapters examined specific Community institutions (the Commission and the European Parliament).[1] This chapter analyses constitutional arrangements in the European Community in their entirety. It puts the points made earlier about the Commission and the European Parliament in the context of Community Treaty arrangements as a whole. As discussed in these previous chapters, when looked at as constitutional arrangements the provisions of the existing Treaties are deeply flawed. New constitutional arrangements are needed in order to take advantage of the new setting in Europe. The time is now ripe to debate what these arrangements should be. This chapter sets out the two main alternatives and looks at their theoretical background as well as the practical issues. The tactical options on how to go about Treaty revision are also briefly mentioned.

---

[1] Above, Chapter 4, 'Europe's Constitutional Deficit', and Chapter 5, 'The Powers of the European Parliament: The Westminster Deficit'. These two chapters include detail on concepts such as subsidiarity as well as details on the Commission and where the review and scrutiny rôle of the European Parliament might be strengthened. These more detailed points are not further discussed in this overview chapter which is concerned with the general thrust of institutional reform in the Community.

II. THE OPPORTUNITY

The collapse of post-war barriers in Europe provides an opportunity to reshape Europe and its institutions. Until now, proposals for the development of the European Community and its institutions have assumed that the wider European setting could be handled as a subject apart from the Community's own institutional evolution. This is no longer possible. The countries of Eastern Europe have made much faster strides towards political pluralism than anticipated; their desire to introduce market-oriented reforms also appears more whole-hearted than earlier seemed likely. Their interest in eventual membership or closer association with the Community has been indicated. European Free Trade Association (EFTA) countries have also made clear their desire to move rapidly towards new arrangements with the Community. As a result, the Community's own evolution must now be seen as part of a wider drawing together in Europe. Not only must the Community's institutional evolution be seen in this wider context, but the agenda of issues will inevitably broaden.

The reshaping that is required in Europe must take place on several different levels. First, the economic motor of the new Europe must be provided by extending the Single Market over time to as many countries as possible. This includes not only the countries of EFTA but also those Eastern European countries that are pursuing market-oriented policies in a pluralist political system. This extended market must also be fully open to global trade and finance.

Secondly, the new security arrangements needed in Europe call for a restructuring of the NATO alliance, for new burden-sharing arrangements between the United States and its European partners and new sharing arrangements among the European members. Within Europe, a distinction needs to be made between the *financial* contributions that a united Germany can eventually make to security arrangements as compared with its *military* contribution in terms of forces. For the economies of France and the UK to carry a larger financial share of Europe's new defence and security arrangements will aggravate economic imbalances in Europe even though they can and must provide a relatively large proportion of its military preparedness. Because of these financial and economic implications, putting Europe's new security arrangements in place will entail not only a reshaping of NATO but also the eventual need for the European Council and the Council of Ministers (or a sub-group of each) to include aspects of defence arrangements among the items on their agenda.

Thirdly, political co-operation in the new Europe requires an overhaul of the constitutional arrangements provided in the Treaties establishing the European Community.

The purpose of the overhaul of the constitutional provisions of the Community Treaties would be:

o to correct the deficiencies of the existing Treaties;

o to provide a flexible basis for co-operation in a wider European setting and with a broader political agenda;

o to place the evolution of Europe's political institutions on a sounder constitutional basis.

Such a review of Community Treaties is now timely. They should be subject to the same scrutiny as other institutional arrangements for the new shape of Europe. The rejection of centralised bureaucratic government in Europe and the connection between market-oriented economies and the assertion of individual liberties is a challenge to many of the existing tenets of the Treaties. In the past, constitutional revision of Community Treaties has been rejected as divisive and unnecessary. Constitutional change, however, can no longer be avoided in Europe's new setting.

III. THE ALTERNATIVES

Two different models for future institutional development in the European Community can be distinguished. The first is a *centralising* vision applicable mainly to existing Community members. It involves building up the central institutions of the Community (in particular the Commission and the Parliament), the putting in place of new central bodies (such as a Second Chamber of the Parliament), and a sharing of power at the centre between Councils, Commission and Parliament. New Treaty provisions would accentuate the normative element of existing articles. Hence the Treaty would be further directed towards an end-state of *'union'* in the sense of an eventual unitary state for the Community grouping. The Court of Justice would play an activist judicial rôle in facilitating institutional and policy evolution to that end.

Under the centralist vision for Europe, Community-level bodies such as the European Parliament would be clearly designated the 'senior' bodies in the political grouping. Conversely, institutions of member-states (such as national parliaments) would be clearly designated as 'junior' bodies. This would be reflected (under the existing primacy of Community law) in new Treaty provisions incorporating centralising definitions of such principles as 'subsidiarity' and by distinguishing between different classes of legislation.

The second model is a *constitutionalist* vision. According to this view, political power in the new Europe should be diffused. This means building on the parliamentary frameworks of member-states as the basic element in political co-operation, with the Heads of Government in the European Council and Ministers of national governments in the Council of Ministers affirmed and strengthened as the key institutions for collective action by the Community and as the key link to other countries in Europe. The constitutional provisions of Community Treaties would be amended and supplemented to provide a framework of rules oriented to preventing the abuse of power by Community-level institutions. The Court of Justice would be referee of the rules, not a maker of laws within an activist frame of reference. 'Union' would be seen as a *process* for achieving collective objectives in Europe, not as an end-goal of a unitary state.

Under the constitutionalist view, a wide array of governmental institutions is seen as necessary for Europe's development. While the European Council and Council of Ministers can provide the capacity for collective action at the Community level, the continued vitality of the parliamentary framework of member-states is seen as an essential safeguard against the accumulation of power in any one central institution or by any group of states. The parliamentary frameworks of member-states provide the key means to keep participatory democracy flourishing, as well as the means to provide for different jurisdictions to test different policies and to reflect different preferences. The aim is to establish the *middle ground* between excessive centralisation where all key powers are concentrated at the Community level and excessive decentralisation under which collective action becomes impossible. Each of these two different visions are set out in further detail below.

IV. THE CENTRALIST VIEW

There are four essential elements in the centralists' view of how the Community should evolve:

(i) the strengthening of institutions at the Community level in a power-sharing arrangement at the centre between Council, Commission and the European Parliament;

(ii) an incorporation of new Treaty provisions demarcating the enlarged sphere of the central bodies;

(iii) supplementary powers for the Court of Justice to adjudicate and enforce these demarcations;

(iv) a change in Community 'decision rules' in order to extend the scope of majority voting and thus make action at the centre less vulnerable to blocking by member-states.

Power-Sharing at the Centre

The lynchpin of the centralist view of Europe's institutional evolution is a sharing of powers at the Community level between Council, Commission and the European Parliament. In order to achieve this objective, enhancements are envisaged for each of these bodies. These enhancements consist of new institutional elements at the centre, accompanied by an enlargement or consolidation of the powers of the Commission and Parliament. The key enhancements are as follows:

o the work of individual ministers in the *Council* would be guided by a new body of 'superministers' (Ministers for European Affairs) sitting as a permanent ministerial body in Brussels;

o the *European Parliament* would receive new legislative powers (the authority to legislate directly) and new financial authority (over the expenditure and revenue side of the Community budget) including the powers to tax;

o the *European Parliament* would, in addition, receive a second chamber, constituted either of members from national parliaments or possibly of the 'superministers' plus deputies who would form the nucleus of a second chamber;

o the *Commission* would have its political direction rôle confirmed[2] and this rôle as well as the Commission's right to initiate and propose on Community matters would be 'validated' by the direct

---

[2] This rôle is encapsulated in Article 155 which expresses the 'guardian' rôle of the Commission as follows:

'In order to ensure the proper functioning and development of the Common Market, the Commission shall:

o ensure that the provisions of this Treaty and the measures taken by the institutions pursuant hereto are applied;

[*Contd. on p. 127*]

election of the Commission's President or by a confirmation voting procedure of the European Parliament.

Demarcation and Adjudication

The second element sought by the centralists is for demarcation provisions to be added to Community Treaties in order to underpin the enlargement of powers involved at the centre. Key among these is the principle of *'subsidiarity'*. This principle would be defined to demarcate between the sphere of responsibility of Community-level bodies and the institutions of member-states in a way that benefits the central institutions. Related Treaty additions are 'subject matter' reserves which would define the subject areas within the jurisdiction (in certain cases the exclusive jurisdiction) of the Community-level bodies, and a distinction between laws applied directly by the centre (sometimes referred to as 'organic laws') and the laws of member-states. 'Organic' laws would have primacy. These additions are interconnected in the sense that the area of jurisdiction for the Community-level bodies would reflect a centralising version of the principle of 'subsidiarity' and might be implemented through 'organic laws'.

The supplementary powers envisaged for the Court of Justice are concomitant with this institutional and Treaty based assertion of powers at the centre. The additional powers would relate to the interpretation of such principles as 'subsidiarity', the application of 'organic' laws emanating from the centre, as well as the adjudication on the competence of central bodies in different subject areas.

Majority Voting

The final element in this centralist view of Community development is a change in the 'decision rules' within the Community—notably in the Councils. The aim would be to make *majority voting* (which currently applies to decisions on the Single Market as well as some other areas) the main or only rule for Council decisions. The unanimity requirement would be restricted, or abolished. The veto convention (the so-called 'Luxembourg compromise') would be set aside. The purpose of these changes in the decision rules would be to reduce the possibility of member-states in the minority being able to block action by the majority.

---

o formulate recommendations or deliver opinions on matters dealt with in this Treaty, if it expressly so provides or if the Commission considers it necessary;

o have its own power of decision and participate in the shaping of measures taken by the Council and by the European Parliament in the manner provided for in this Treaty.'

For reasons of both presentation and tactics, the four key ingredients in the centralist view of institutional development may be presented in their component parts rather than as a whole. However, they should be seen together as a package or as an inevitable and intended sequence. The change in the decision rules makes the enhanced powers of the central bodies easier to invoke; the demarcation definitions enlarge the sphere of their operation and the Court of Justice enforces the new legal basis.

Constitutionalist Objections

The constitutionalist has three main objections to this package.

First, the sharing of powers at the centre will inevitably lead to *confusion* as to which body should be held responsible for a particular set of policies. This erodes the value of the electoral vote in the democratic process because the effectiveness of voting depends on the elector being able to allocate responsibility and to vote to change those responsible if the voter disagrees with the policies. The confusion of responsibility also gives interest groups much more play in the political system because they have greater opportunity amidst an unstable jostling for power and because their actions are less easy to identify. Indeed, because of the erosion of the value of the vote, the individual elector has to find other ways of channelling his views and interest groups provide the next best channel. It is, however, very much a second-best solution. Interest groups can give expression only to a narrow range of a voter's views; the political process becomes murky, and money (needed both to organise and persuade) becomes a much larger feature of the political system. If the central bodies are prone to regulate economic interests, then money interests become that much more prominent in the system because their vital interests are at stake. All of these features are characteristics of the American system of government but they are not desirable either in the United States or in Europe. They lead to a cynicism about the political process and a further demotivation of the voter. Low voter participation rates in the United States are no coincidence. Europe has a chance to avoid the blemishes of the US democratic process. The opportunity to find alternatives should be taken.[3]

---

[3] The centralist may attempt to justify the sharing of powers between Council, Commission and Parliament as a form of 'separation of powers'. It is, however, a travesty of that concept. For a discussion of what is intended by a separation of powers, see, for example, F. A. Hayek, *New Studies in Philosophy, Politics, Economics and the History of Ideas*, London: Routledge and Kegan Paul, 1978.

A second objection of the constitutionalist is to the key rôle accorded to the *bureaucratic* element in the power-sharing arrangements proposed by the centralist—namely, the Commission. The apologists point to the important rôle played by all bureaucrats within national and international frameworks. However, the powers accorded the Commission extend far beyond the customary. The 'guardian' role reflected in Article 155, the numerous references in the Treaties to the initiating and proposing functions of the Commission and its 'middleman' position in the procedures of the European Parliament, go well beyond the civil service and agency functions that are appropriate for bureaucracies. The political direction rôle accorded the Commission reflects a distrust of the democratic process (understandable in the early post-war period) and a belief that a guiding 'enlightened élite' has a rôle to play outside democratic channels. For the constitutionalist such élitism has no place. Democracy may not provide the most enlightened or efficient forms of government but it enshrines other more important values. The proposal to have the Head of the Commission directly elected or validated by an indirect electoral process only aggravates the problem. It introduces a personal element into the central bodies of the Community which is avoided by the rotating leadership among the group of elected Heads of Governments in the Council. It raises the possibility of the Commission obtaining a pre-eminent rôle at the centre by virtue of superior cohesion in relation to the Parliament and the Heads of Government. This would take Europe a step towards an American presidential system with all the drawbacks of over-personalised government without any of the safeguards of the American constitution. For the constitutionalist, the direction of change must be in the opposite direction—to rid treaty arrangements of the political rôle accorded the Commission.

The third objection of the constitutionalist is that the new Treaty provisions proposed by the centralist and intended to demarcate the enlarged sphere of the central bodies and the rôle of the Court of Justice, will work not to safeguard other jurisdictions but to *emasculate* them. The distinctions offered by such concepts as 'subsidiarity', 'organic laws' and 'subject matter reserves' are vague, subjective and open-ended.[4]

---

[4] For a recent expression of legal reservations, see 'Note by Counsel to the Speaker—Subsidiarity', in *Minutes of Evidence*, 'The Operation of the Single European Act', House of Commons Foreign Affairs Committee, 17 January 1990.

They will be defined in a way to permit a gradual or rapid further assertion of power at the centre. The problem is accentuated by the rôle accorded the Court of Justice. As noted by a former British permanent representative to the Community, 'the Court's judgements, rather naturally tend in the direction of strengthening the rôle of Community law'.[5] For the constitutionalist, the purpose of Treaty revisions would be to correct any such bias. Instead of the Treaties providing a framework for interpretative activism by the Court with a centralising tendency, the aim of revisions should be to emphasise the rôle of the Court as an impartial arbiter.

These objections of the constitutionalist to the centralising vision of institutional development in the Community are not necessarily fatal. As noted at the outset, the member-states of Europe require an increased capacity to act collectively; institutional arrangements are needed to bring together a wider grouping of European states in various forms of association or membership; and a broader political agenda may also need to be addressed by the Community. It is therefore incumbent on the constitutionalist to set out an alternative pattern of development that will fulfil these objectives.

V. THE CONSTITUTIONALIST APPROACH

The constitutionalist approach is built around the following key elements:

o The primacy of the *European Council* supported by the Council of Ministers for arriving at collective decisions in the Community would be brought out clearly. New arrangements might be needed in addition so that the Councils can bring Heads of Governments and Ministers of other European countries into closer association. The Commission's functions would be restricted to a civil service and agency rôle.

o Explicit recognition would be given in the Treaties to the *parliamentary systems* of member-states as the source of authority for Heads of Government and Ministers at the European Council/ Council of Ministers level. The function of the parliaments of member-states to act as chambers of debate and scrutiny in respect of issues for collective decisions to be taken at the Councils (as well

---

[5] Sir Michael Butler, *Europe: More than a Continent*, London: Heinemann, 1986.

as to perform as Assemblies for issues concerning only the particular member-state) would also be explicitly recognised in the Treaties.

o The role of the European Parliament would be defined as a *forum* for additional support for the Assemblies of member-states for the review and scrutiny of policies undertaken by the Community collectively. By virtue of its proximity to Commission, Council of Ministers and COREPER, the review rôle would usefully focus on the economic effectiveness of Community spending programmes and as a check on any abuse of powers by the Commission in addition to its current pre-legislative focus.

o Decision rules of the Community Treaties would be extended in order to incorporate a right of *veto* for member-states and (probably more importantly in practice) to incorporate provisions enabling a member-state in a minority to opt out of a collective decision. The opting out provision could be expressed in the form of different types of constitutional reserves (executive, legislative and popular).

o Treaty provisions relating to the setting in which the Court of Justice operates would be amended to ensure that it functioned as an *impartial arbiter* of Community processes rather than encouraging a law-making tendency towards promoting an end-state of 'union'. Provisions enabling it to take more effective action against the abuse of powers would be strengthened.

o New economic provisions might be included in the Treaties to provide a further defence against abuses of powers and to guard against an accretion of power by the Community acting collectively. These would be expressed in terms of *constitutional limits* on the size of the Community budget (at, say, a fixed proportion of the GNP of member-states), and an obligation on the monetary authorities to keep inflation in the 0-2 per cent a year range. (This is analogous to the Bundesbank Articles which enjoin it to preserve the value of the currency.)

Constitutional Solution:
Collective Action *and* Diffusion of Power

The overriding purpose of these arrangements would be to establish the middle ground between the necessity for member-states to be able to take collective action on a broad agenda of issues as a Community

TABLE 1

ALTERNATIVE INSTITUTIONAL STRUCTURES

CONSTITUTIONALIST		CENTRALIST
POLITICAL DIRECTION		
European Council (Heads of Governments) Council of Ministers	SHARED	{ European Council/Council of Ministers[1] Commission European Parliament[2]
SOURCE OF AUTHORITY		
Parliaments of Member States National Electorates	MIXED	{ National Parliaments/ Electorates for Councils Treaty Based for Commission[3] Euro Electorate for European Parliament
SCRUTINY & REVIEW (INCLUDING LEGAL BASE)		
Court of Justice European Parliament Parliaments of Member States (Part Function)		Court of Justice[4] European Parliament (Part Function)

[1] Probably 'permanent' at deputy PM level with own secretariat.

[2] With power to legislate directly, and budget authority to raise revenues (tax), borrow, guarantee and accept contingent obligations.

[3] To be validated by a direct or indirect election procedure.

[4] Within context of demarcation devices below.

[5] Sub-agencies may be necessary to distinguish between exercise of administrative and quasi-judicial functions.

---

while preserving the vitality of different jurisdictions. The European Council and Council of Ministers would have the capacity to act collectively on all issues but the parliamentary systems of member-states would have a pivotal rôle in providing a diffusion of power among different jurisdictions. (See Table 1 and Charts A and B.)

The trimming of the powers of the Commission together with the extension of the review and scrutiny rôle of the European Parliament would help guard against bureaucratic centralisation. The composition avoids the horizontal distinction in structures between senior bodies at

TABLE 1 (Continued)

CONSTITUTIONALIST	CENTRALIST
NEW CONSTITUTIONAL FEATURES	
Decision Rules	*Decision Rules*
* Veto Power (Luxembourg Compromise)	* Majority Voting on Most/ All Subjects
* Opting Out Provisions (Executive, Legislative and Popular Reserves)	
Demarcation Devices	*Demarcation Devices*
Reformulate Terms of Reference of Community Institutions	* Subsidiarity * Organic Laws * Subject Matter Reserves
Against Abuse of Powers	*Against Abuse of Powers*
* New Ultra Vires Provisions	
* Limits on Community Budget (i.e. Not to exceed X% of GNP)	
* Monetary Stipulation (Value of Currencies to be Maintained)	
CIVIL SERVICE AND AGENCY	
Commission (Exclusive Function)[5] COREPER (Civil Services of Member States)	Commission (Part Function)

Note: This Table summarises the main points of difference between the constitutionalist framework for a wider European setting and the centralist structure. It does not go into such detail as, for example, how 'subsidiarity' might be defined, nor does it attempt to give, for example, a reformulation of Article 155 on the terms of reference of the Commission. The point is a more general one—namely, that advocates of both centralist and constitutionalist alternatives are calling into question basic constitutional issues which should now be addressed under the auspices of the European Council.

the Community level and institutions of member-states relegated to a junior level which is made by the centralists.

The changes envisaged by the constitutionalist in the decision-rules of the Community are an integral feature of the balance being sought between collective decision-taking and diffused powers. The veto power is one for highly restricted use. It ensures that all members go along with a policy of fundamental importance (or possibly a constitutional change). However, it involves the cost of blocking all members if a single member does not concur. The opting-out provision is a more flexible device. It enhances the incentive for the majority in the Councils to obtain unanimous consent. If there is an immovable minority view, however, the majority can proceed in their own jurisdictions. Different preferences among different jurisdictions are preserved. Different policies can be tested and compared. It recognises that virtue may lie in divergencies rather than in harmonisation.

Would ministerial Councils abuse their power if clearly given the key rôle? There are many restraints: their members would need to retain their majorities in national parliaments; the Treaties would contain new provisions against the abuse of powers; and the Court of Justice would be placed in an impartial setting. The European Parliament too would exercise a more extensive review and scrutiny rôle. In addition, rotating leadership in the Councils guards against personalisation of power.

An important objective of this structure is to facilitate a widening of the Community. The suggestion by the present head of the Commission (Jacques Delors) is for a Europe of concentric circles. The present Community (or an even smaller nucleus) would accept to be bound by the centralist model. Other states of Europe would arrange themselves in different degrees of tightness around the perimeter. This division of Europe's member-states into first-class, second-class and third-class members is repugnant. What historical basis exists to distinguish between Belgium, Austria and Hungary as first-, second- and third-class Europeans respectively? The problem arises from the narrow bureaucratic vision of the centralist. By contrast, the constitutionalist model, with collective action at the ministerial level and the institutional bed-rock remaining with member-states, provided a more robust framework for the flexible relationships which can now begin to be extended throughout Europe.

VI. THEORY

Underlying the two different models of centralist evolution for Community institutions or the constitutionalist alternative, are different theoretical considerations. The centralist posits a close relationship between optimum market size and the optimum size of political unit and identifies each with the present Community grouping. Phrases such as 'political unity must follow economic unity' reflect this kind of postulate. The constitutionalist is more concerned with processes than with end-states, rejects the kind of correlation between market size and optimum political unit size advocated by the centralist and sees optimum market size and flexible political arrangements extending well beyond the present Community. There are three main considerations underlying this theoretical debate and each is outlined below.

1. The Range of Public Choice

The first relates to public choice. Interdependence among Europe's economies means that certain policies can be offered only at the level of collective action of all member-states, or can most effectively be offered there. For example, it is widely accepted that external trade policies are best set by the Community collectively. Defence and security arrangements are a good example of policies which can best be offered at the collective level, which are not offered by the present Community but may need to be addressed in the future. The centralist draws the conclusion that the centre of gravity for political direction must therefore be at the Community level and that the key policy levers be exercised by the Community's central institutions.

The constitutionalist starts from the same point of departure. It is accepted that public choice is enriched by policies that can be offered through collective action by the Community. For this reason, in the constitutionalist model the Councils are the key body for collective action, with the potential to act collectively over a broad range of policies.

However, the constitutionalist also qualifies his view of the desirability of exercising public choice at the Community level. The number of public policies that are best offered or can only be offered at the level of collective action is limited. Furthermore, some policies which may become offerable at the Community level may be undesirable (for example, the renewed scope for market interventionist policies). Moreover, once powers are established at the centre they may be used to usurp control over other policies that do not have to be offered at the level of collective action. In respect of this last point, it is bureaucratic empire building that is a key concern of the constitutionalist but not the only concern.

Because of these qualifications, the model of the constitutionalist strips the Commission of its rôle of political direction. It also emphasises the necessity for strong constitutional rules against the abuse of power, including budget and monetary rules designed to make an assertion of powers at the centre more difficult, as well as to check the in-built bias of politicians to offer policies without the means of payment. In short, the constitutionalist attempts the difficult balancing act between according the Councils the power to adopt collective policies wherever they may best be offered, combined with strong constitutional rules against the abuse of power and tendencies for power to accrete at the centre. The proposed balance looks back to the separation of powers of classical liberalism[6] between specific legislative acts (agreed by the Councils) and general rules of political conduct (enshrined in the new provisions envisaged for the Constitution). It also rests crucially on the diffusion of powers achieved by maintaining the prerogatives of the democratic systems of member-states.

2. Clubs, Unions and Decision Rules

The second theoretical consideration relates to the effectiveness of collective action in clubs, alliances and unions and, by analogy, in the Community. Broadly speaking, a union is likely to be more effective than an alliance because it can exercise 'coercion' over its reluctant members (the 'coercion' is accepted voluntarily through the decision rules of the union). Thus the well-known problem of 'free riders' is avoided. The centralist advocates the desirability of this kind of 'coercion' in the Community and it is reflected in the preference for the decision-rule of majority voting. The terminology of 'union' in the preamble of the existing Treaties is used to justify this general approach to collective action by the Community as well as the centralists' frequent desire to see an eventual end-destination of a unitary state of Europe.

The decision-rules of the constitutionalist (veto and opting-out provisions) accept the efficiency loss that results from a situation where 'coercion' may not always be exercisable. But this efficiency loss is regarded as more than offset by the value attributed to the preservation of different jurisdictions. These enable different policy preferences to be exercised and different policies to be tested out. It is held that Europe's history gives ample reason to support cultural diversity, and to avoid the consequences of majorities persistently overruling minorities. Moreover, minorities may be 'right'. The testing of different policies in different jurisdictions is likely to be to the benefit of all. Dissonance may discourage bureaucratic minds but it reflects the functioning of a healthy democratic system.

---

[6] Hayek, *op. cit.*

3. Separating Preferences

A third theoretical consideration is the postulate that democratic processes are best served by institutions that distinguish between policies on offer at the collective level and institutions that deal with other policies that do not have to be taken collectively. These distinctions are reflected in the division between the senior-level central bodies of the Community and the junior-level institutions in member-states proposed by the centralist. The centralist holds that by dividing a broad range of policies into two or more narrower and distinct ranges, the scope for divergences in political preferences is diminished, the need for 'coercion' is reduced, and democratic preferences can be expressed more clearly.

The constitutionalist rejects these propositions in the context of Europe for three reasons. First, because the suppliers of policies at the senior level will face in a wider Europe an even more heterogeneous electorate than today, the senior bodies at the centre will be under two undesirable pressures. One will be to offer policy options in a 'weak' form in electoral situations, simplifying the message and reducing political debate to the 10-second TV 'sound bites' familiar from US Presidential politics. The other will be the pressure to introduce policies to harmonise and encourage a more homogeneous society. The constitutionalist regards neither of these tendencies as desirable. The constitutionalist looks to diversity in Europe as a source of creativity, and important also for the sense of an individual's identity in a broader European society.

Secondly, the supposed advantages of separating preferences will, according to the constitutionalist, be nullified by the confusion of power at the senior level under centralist proposals which further erode the electoral process. It will be special interests that will be catered for and courted by the centre.

Thirdly, but not the least consideration, those bodies that will become 'junior' bodies under the centralist model (national parliaments) happen to have been the bulwark of freedom in Europe up to the present. They may not always have worked, and in Eastern Europe, democratic practices have to be re-established. Nevertheless, if their rôle is eroded, it will not easily be regained. If democratic practices do not flourish in individual member-states, they are unlikely to flourish at the centre.

As indicated above, purely theoretical considerations are fairly

[Contd. on p. 140]

137

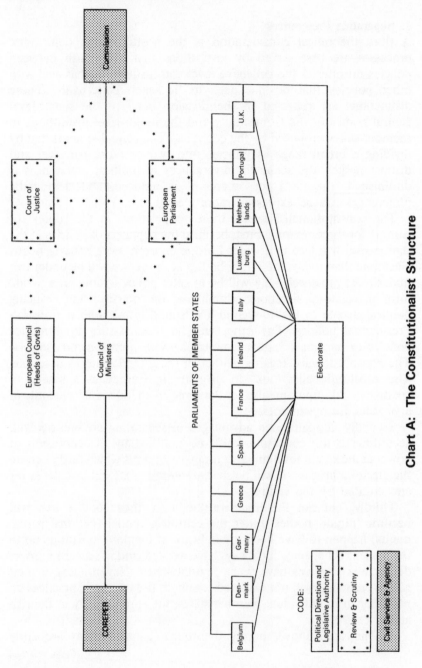

Chart A: The Constitutionalist Structure

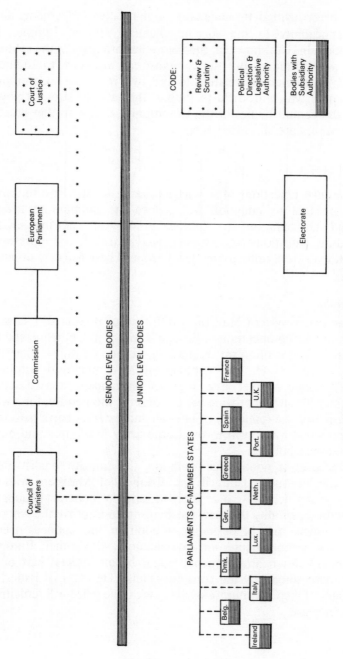

Chart B: The Centralist Structure

quickly overwhelmed by pragmatic or normative judgements about their applicability to the specific characteristics of Europe. The constitutionalist can show that the theoretical premises of the centralist are not well founded. But the centralist can also turn to additional practical considerations relating to the two models of Community development which are held to support the case for stronger powers among the central bodies of the Community. These further practical considerations are discussed next.

VII. PRACTICAL ISSUES

The centralist objections of a practical nature to the constitutionalist model are that its adoption will reduce the momentum towards increased co-operation in Europe, erode part of the existing Community patrimony (the *acquis communautaire*), and represents a tacit nationalism harmful to the new Europe. These fears are discussed below.

Momentum

The fear that a system built on a diffusion of powers will slow the momentum for co-operation in Europe is rooted in a bureaucratic bias which sees interventionism as guiding Europe's future rather than market dynamics. On the contrary, it is competition within an extended Single Market area, together with open external trading arrangements that will provide basic economic momentum for a wider Europe. It was the reduction of internal and external barriers to trade which provided dynamism to the Community in the past and not its interventionist policies.

At the level of political co-operation, the constitutionalist model equips the European Council and Council of Ministers with the capacity to act decisively over a broad range of policies. It does not exclude the possibility that new mechanisms to improve the workings of the Councils may be desirable. In addition, the Councils need to make new arrangements for co-operation with other European governments. Such arrangements would be an integral part of the development sought by the constitutionalist. On external issues, the advantages of the Community speaking with one voice will remain and indeed increase.

The *Acquis Communautaire*

The doctrine of the *acquis communautaire* (or patrimony) states that once a function or power has been obtained at the Community level, it should never be relinquished. It is a pernicious doctrine. It encourages rigidities which will hinder Europe's integration rather than help it. The new situation in Europe requires new policies and new institutional structures. A leading example of past Community policies that have outlived their time is the Common Agricultural Policy (CAP). Within the existing Community, it benefits narrow interests at the expense of the population as a whole; it encourages financial excess, supports arbitrary resource transfers and a spiral of bureaucratic regulation, fraud and enforcement. Externally it is damaging to open trading arrangements. In the context of a larger Community, the countries of Eastern Europe with their much larger proportion of population in agriculture dependent on agricultural income, with much of their comparative advantage in agricultural produce, need unrestricted access to the markets of the Community and not the barrier of CAP.

The idea that old functions should always be sustained and new policies always additional is a bureaucrat's dream. The concept of the *acquis communautaire* is a doctrine invented by bureaucrats for the benefit of bureaucrats. It is a doctrine correctly spurned in the constitutionalist model. Different jurisdictions in an open-market setting will provide a framework for competition, creative diversity, change and a rightful rejection of the self-serving biases of centralised bureaucracies.

Nationalism

There are two quite different issues involved under the rubric of nationalism. The first is how to accommodate, within the context of the new Europe, *imbalances* between member-states (in particular, the concern expressed by some about the weight of Germany which on a unified basis accounts for between 25 and 30 per cent of existing Community GNP). The centralist reverts to the original ECSC idea of clearly tilting the centre of gravity in political arrangements towards supranational institutions at the centre of the Community. The constitutionalist sees the issue as the more classical liberal one of how to preserve the rights of minorities *vis-à-vis* a majority or a dominant partner. The diffusion of power, related decision-rules and constitutional provisions against the abuse of power are therefore seen by the

141

constitutionalist as providing a surer way of dealing with imbalances. Diffusion is not nationalism under a new guise. On the contrary, a more robust framework for increased co-operation in a wider European setting is a key objective of the constitutionalist model.

The second issue is that those supporting centralist development frequently see a unitary state of Europe as the *end-goal* of European union. The constitutionalist emphasis on a diffusion of power is thus seen as a hindrance to this eventual goal. The constitutionalist regards 'union' as a process of co-operation—a unitary state is not sought. Those who support the idea of a unitary state of Europe see it as some kind of 'middle way' between Soviet socialism and American capitalism. They forget that freedoms in Europe have been made possible in this century largely because of American support and because of the steadfastness of the post-war Atlantic Alliance. The emotional appeal to a unitary state of Europe is also regarded with distrust by the constitutionalist. It plays heavily to the same emotionalism in politics that led to the evil excesses of nationalism in the past.

A further point that is relevant in this context is that democratic diversity strikes the outside observer differently from the way it is seen by the inside participant. The outside observer wishes to deal with a cohesive unit. Thus European countries and Japan have difficulties in dealing with the democratic processes of decision-taking in the United States. The mirror image is the advocacy by successive US administrations of 'unity' in Europe. Neither party should forget that democracy is about the diversity of ideas, the tolerance of differences, the competition between different approaches—and not about co-hesion. Cohesion reflects the historical chance of a homogeneous society or the shadow of autocracy. The US administration should be careful not to misinterpret the constitutional debate in Europe.

Future Discussions

A final practical issue of importance to both centralists and constitutionalists is how to embark on the constitutional discussions now required in the Community. The Inter Governmental Conference arranged for December 1990 in connection with talks on monetary union is one occasion at which institutional issues may be taken up. However, to take proper advantage of the new opportunities in Europe, the constitutional discussions need to be wide-ranging. A second possibility is for the European Council to make separate arrangements for preparation and discussion of broader constitutional issues. Such an effort should clearly take place under the auspices of the European Council and not under the Commission with its vested interest in particular outcomes. Such a broadening of the constitutional review would be timely.[7]

Discussions about Europe's constitutional future will be divisive. Precisely because of this, they have been largely avoided in the past. A pragmatic 'muddling through' has seemed preferable. The time has come when this so-called 'pragmatism' is no longer appropriate. What seems like a series of small self-contained steps can produce the wrong overall result because of a neglect of the larger picture. There is a new situation in Europe which requires a more far-reaching response if the opportunities are to be taken. As remarked by Professor Buchanan in the context of constitutional reform in the United States,

> 'I am convinced that the social interrelationships that emerge from continued pragmatic and incremental ... response, informed by no philosophical precepts, is neither sustainable nor worthy of man's best efforts'.[8]

The opportunities now available to reshape Europe and its institutions require no less than Europe's best efforts.

VIII. CONCLUSIONS

The 1990s open with an opportunity to create and put in place new arrangements for political and economic co-operation in Europe which will cover a much wider grouping of European states and a broader agenda. In order to take advantage of this opportunity, new constitutional arrangements are required in the Community. The model offered by the constitutionalists provides for collective action on a broad range of topics on a Europe-wide basis by emphasising the rôle of the European Council supported by the Council of Ministers. At the same time, the model relies on democratic practices in the member-states as a way of diffusing power, making sure that government remains close to the people and that different preferences can be

---

[7] Subsequent to the original publication of this chapter (as *IEA Inquiry* No. 17, March 1990), the European Council agreed to establish a second Inter Governmental Conference on political union.

[8] James M. Buchanan, *The Limits of Liberty*, Chicago: University of Chicago Press, 1975.

expressed and exercised in different jurisdictions. It is a more challenging model than that of the centralist. It is an easy temptation to respond to the uncertainties of the present situation with proposals to build up central institutions. It would be the wrong course to follow. The division of institutions between senior- and junior-level bodies will weaken democratic roots in Europe, and open the risks of bureaucratic, personalised government remote from the people, and where interest groups will have a special advantage to press their particular claims.

The constitutionalist model offers the best hope for a new flowering of democratic diversity in as wide as possible a European setting. In discussions with its European partners, Britain should firmly reject any step towards a centralist Europe. Instead it should take the lead and encourage its partners in Europe to broaden their vision and look to build a new constitutional basis for a new Europe.

THE AUTHORS

James M. Buchanan is a Nobel Laureate and the Harris University Professor and Advisory General Director, Center for Study of Public Choice, George Mason University, Fairfax, Virginia. He was formerly Professor of Economics and Director of the Center for Study of Public Choice at the Virginia Polytechnic Institute, Blacksburg, Virginia; Professor of Economics at Florida State University, 1951-56; University of Virginia (and Director of the Thomas Jefferson Center for Political Economy), 1956-68; University of California at Los Angeles, 1968-69.

Professor Buchanan is the author of numerous works on aspects of the economics of politics and public choice, including (with Gordon Tullock) *The Calculus of Consent* (1962); *Public Finance in Democratic Process* (1967); *Demand and Supply of Public Goods* (1968); *The Limits of Liberty: Between Anarchy and Leviathan* (1975); and (with Richard E. Wagner) *Democracy in Deficit: The Political Legacy of Lord Keynes* (1977). He is a member of the IEA's Advisory Council. The IEA has published his *The Inconsistencies of the National Health Service* (Occasional Paper 7, 1965); (with Richard E. Wagner and John Burton) *The Consequences of Mr Keynes* (Hobart Paper 78, 1978); 'From Private Preference to Public Philosophy: The Development of Public Choice', in *The Economics of Politics* (Readings 18, 1978); 'Our Times: Past, Present, and Future' in *The Unfinished Agenda* (1986); and 'Post-Reagan Political Economy', in *Reaganomics and After* (IEA Readings 28, 1989).

Victoria Curzon Price studied at Geneva University and the Graduate Institute of International Studies in Geneva, where she obtained her academic degrees. There she also settled down, married, had three children—and embarked on an academic career.

Her thesis, entitled *The Essentials of Economic Integration* (Macmillan, 1972), was about the European Free Trade Association (EFTA). Here she claimed that freeing trade was 'the essential' element in trying to create an integrated economic space and that harmonisation (then being pursued with enthusiasm by the European Economic Community) was not necessary. Strangely enough, this

145

theme is once more to the fore, this time as official European Community policy. Her 1988 Wincott Memorial Lecture, *1992: Europe's Last Chance? From Common Market to Single Market* (published by the IEA as Occasional Paper 81) charts some of the implications of this 'new approach' to economic integration. This was followed by her 'Three Models of European Integration', in *Whose Europe?* (IEA Readings 29, 1989).

Victoria Curzon Price is Professor of Economics at the Institut Universitaire d'Etudes Européennes (University of Geneva) and Visiting Faculty Member at the International Management Institute, Geneva.

Karl Otto Pöhl has been President of the Deutsche Bundesbank since 1980 (previously Vice-President, 1977-79). Born in Hanover in 1929, he is an economist by training, educated at the University of Göttingen. He was Head of Department for Economic Research, IFO-Institute, Munich, 1955-60; an economic journalist in Bonn from 1961-67; member of the Management Board of the Federal Association of German Banks, Cologne, 1968-69; Head of Department, Federal Ministry of Economic Affairs, 1970-71; Head of the Economic and Fiscal Policy Department, Federal Chancellor's Office, 1971-72; State Secretary of the Federal Ministry of Finance, 1972-77; Chairman of the EEC Monetary Committee, 1976-77; German Governor of the International Monetary Fund and the Bank for International Settlements, since 1980; Chairman of the Council of Central Banks; and a Director of the Kreditanstalt für Wiederaufbau, Frankfurt am Main. Dr Pöhl delivered the third IEA Special Lecture in London in July 1990.

Frank Vibert was educated at Oundle School and the University of Oxford (First Class Honours in PPE, 1963. He was a Senior Research Fellow at the Institute of Economic Affairs, 1989-90, and is now its Deputy Director. He has been a Senior Fellow with the World Institute for Development Economics Research at the United Nations University in Helsinki, Finland, since 1989. He was formerly a Principal Administrator, Economics and Statistics Department, at the Organisation for Economic Co-operation and Development, Paris, 1965-67; Program Officer, Senior Economist, Adviser and Senior Adviser with the World Bank, Washington DC, 1967-87. His publications include two WIDER Study Group Reports, *Debt Reduction* (No. 3), and *Foreign Portfolio Investment in Emerging Equity Markets* (No. 5).

IEA PUBLICATIONS
Subscription Service

An annual subscription is the most convenient way to obtain our publications. Every title we produce in all our regular series will be sent to you immediately on publication and without further charge, representing a substantial saving.

Individual subscription rates*

Britain: £30·00 p.a. including postage.
£28·00 p.a. if paid by Banker's Order.
£18·00 p.a. to teachers and students who pay *personally.*

Europe: £30·00 p.a. including postage.

South America: £40·00 p.a. or equivalent.

Other Countries: Rates on application. In most countries subscriptions are handled by local agents. Addresses are available from the IEA.

* These rates are *not* available to companies or to institutions.

To: The Treasurer, Institute of Economic Affairs,
2 Lord North Street, Westminster,
London SW1P 3LB

I should like to subscribe from ....

I enclose a cheque/postal order for:

☐ £30·00

☐ £18·00   I am a teacher/student at ....

....

☐ Please send a Banker's Order form.

☐ Please send an invoice.

☐ Please charge my credit card:

Please tick ☐ **VISA** ☐ ◣ ☐ **AMERICAN EXPRESS** ☐ ◀❶▶

Card No: ☐☐☐☐☐☐☐☐☐☐☐☐☐☐☐☐☐☐

In addition I would like to purchase the following previously published titles:

....

....

Name ....

Address ....

....

.... Post Code ....

} BLOCK LETTERS PLEASE

Signed .... Date ....

RPE33